SEE THE WORLD AS A FIVE LAYERED CAKE

SEE THE WORLD AS A
FIVE LAYERED CAKE

Amit Goswami, PhD

©Amit Goswami 2021

All rights reserved
All rights reserved by author. No part of this publication may be reproduced, stored in a retrieval system or transmitted in any form or by any means, electronic, mechanical, photocopying, recording or otherwise, without the prior permission of the author.

Although every precaution has been taken to verify the accuracy of the information contained herein, the author and publisher assume no responsibility for any errors or omissions. No liability is assumed for damages that may result from the use of information contained within.

First Published in February 2021

ISBN: 978-93-5427-439-8

Cover Design:
Debabrata Dey Biswas

Typographic Design:
Tanya Raj Upadhyay

To all people everywhere who want to explore reality

Preface

I began to write this book a little reluctantly, because I discovered the theory of experience I posit here in the 1980s, and wrote and published a definitive book on it in 1993, *The Self-aware Universe*. The following year the philosopher Robert Chalmers made the problem of conscious experience famous by calling it a "hard problem". I have since presented my theory in most of my books, because it is so basic to the quantum worldview. In spite of that, people keep talking about the *hard problem* but not the solution.

My wife used to joke about this. A woman goes to a tailor to get her wedding dress stitched but she wants the tailor to use fifty yards of fabric. The Tailor is surprised. "Madam, will due apology, you need much less." The woman says, "You don't understand. My fiancé is a consciousness researcher. He would rather explore than find."

However, the theory of experience presented in *The Self-Aware Universe* was incomplete. Now that we have started a post-graduate degree-offering Institution, Quantum Activism Vishwalayam—in Jaipur, India for teaching transformation—quantum style--the necessity for a book on the theory of experiences alone has become clear. Hence, I present this book.

The book exposes not only the theory of experience to readers, but also the fact that the Upanishads discovered the essence of this theory some 7000 years ago. However, I want to emphasize this difference between the quantum and the Upanishadic point of view: whereas the Upanishads saw reality as five sheaths of ignorance, quantum science does not. Quantum science looks at the five layers of reality more as a five layered cake to enjoy as you penetrate the layers and discover greater and greater happiness.

What will you get out of reading this book? I paraphrase from chapter 1 and hope the following changes will happen in your understanding of ~~the~~ reality:

1. Reality comes to us as a layered cake. Each layer acts like a sheath of ignorance only until you understand it.
2. The first layer comes to you as external experience and is perhaps the biggest camouflage of reality one ever saw. However, an unbiased examination of quantum physics is all you need to see through the camouflage.
3. The other layers are based on experiences within you. Quantum science will help you navigate the darkness to light.
4. As you eat your cake layer by layer, the darkness of your ignorance gives way to the light of wisdom. Ideally, eating would consist of incorporating the wisdom in your body and/or brain. But even conceptual understanding would entail a partial clearance of the darkness.
5. As you are undoubtedly aware, you and human beings in general do behave like mechanical robots some of the time. As you penetrate the cake layer by layer, a surprise awaits you. You will discover new creative freedom and an expansion of consciousness with an increasing ability to include others—a very non-robotic behavior that produces happiness.
6. Concomitantly, the more you use your creative freedom, the further you will penetrate the cake of reality with increasing happiness (the Sanskrit word is *ananda*) and intelligence.

Table of Contents

1. It's a Challenge Seeing the world as a Five Layered Anything 1
   - I A Story in the Upanishads 1
   - II The Material Realism/Monistic Idealism Debate 8
   - III Quantum Science 16
2. The First Layer of the Reality cake: The Physical World and Quantum Physics that Governs it 20
   - I An Introduction to Quantum Physics 20
   - II Particles and Waves... 24
   - III More Quantum Paradoxes...................................... 34
   - IV The Denouement: My discovery of the Science behind Experience.. 39
   - V The Camouflage the Physical Layer Creates............ 43
3. Inward Journey: The Quantum Science of Experience 46
   - I Tangled Hierarchy 46
   - II The Quantum Self and the Ego 53
   - III Subtle Experiences... 56
   - IV Descartes' Errors and the Importance of Intuition 60
   - V The Tibetan Book of the Dead is Correct; it is your job to prove it 64
   - VI The Quantum Psychophysical Parallelism............... 66
   - VII Does Quantum Physics Apply to us?..................... 70
4. The Second Layer of Manifest Reality: The Vital Body... 73
   - I Liturgical Fields 73
   - II Scientific Explanation of Chakras and Chakra Psychology 81
   - III Why fear Suppresses love and love happens when we let go of fear... 86
   - IV The Male-Female Difference 89

5. Discovering the Third Layer of Reality: Mind with Meaning 91
   I What is Mind? 91
   II Is Mind Brain? 96
   III The Quantum Nature of the Mind 100
   IV Are Thoughts Possibilities of Meaning before We Experience them? Marcel's Experiment 103
   V Zen Mind, Quantum Physics, and Creativity 105
6. Try to Create the Inner Reality You Like and Live there or Integrate the Inner and the Outer? Schizophrenia, Drugs, and Dreams 118
   I Brain in Transition 118
   II Can Drugs Help with Consciousness Raising? 121
   III Is Schizophrenia a Failure to act Creatively? 125
   IV Dreams: Integrating the Inner and the Outer 127
7. Penetrating the Mental and Vital Layers 134
   I Penetrating sheaths: What does that Mean? 134
   II The Quantum Principles of Transformation 136
8. Discovering the Fourth Layer: The World of the Archetypes 146
   I Intuitions and Archetypes 146
   II The Nine Major Archetypes 149
   III The Quantum Nature of Archetypes 151
   IV The Archetype of Truth 152
   V The Archetypes of Abundance 155
   VI The Archetypes of Abundance and Power: Is it Possible to Eliminate Elitism? 159
   VII The Archetype of Love 163
   VIII Good and Evil: the two Faces of the Archetype of Goodness 165
   IX The Archetype of Beauty 167
   X The Archetype of Justice 169

    XI The Archetype of Wholeness and Healthcare in A Quantum Society 171
    XII The Archetypes of Love, Wholeness, and Self 174
    XIII See the World as a Vale for Soul-making 176
    XIV How is it like Living as a soul? 178

9. Who am I? The Two Faces of the Self 180
    I The Ego: How the Self Acquires I—me Polarity 180
    II The Importance of Intuition as a Conduit for Experiencing the Quantum Self 182
    III Is the Holy Spirit a Fantasy of the Religious Mind? 185
    IV An Imaginary Dialog about the relation of I and Me 188
    V Self Realisation: the penetration of the fourth Supramental Sheath 191

10. The Fifth Layer: "Experiencing" the Unconscious in Suchness 193
    I Experiencing the Fifth Layer: *Nirvikalpa Samadhi* 193
    II The Delayed-Choice Experiment in the Macro world 195
    III The State of Consciousness called *Turiya* 197
    IV Why Enlightenment? 200

11. The Quantum Worldview 203
12. Further Reading 216

Chapter 1

It's a Challenge Seeing the world as a Five Layered Anything

I
A Story in the Upanishads

The title of the book should intrigue you, oh ye of modern times. Why should we think of the world as a five-layered anything? Why five layers when we obviously live in one material world? The other layers are non-material, subtle; they are easy to miss. A story from the Upanishads written some seven thousand years ago clarifies.

A curious boy asks his father—a wise teacher, "Father, what is the nature of reality?" The father, though pleased with the question does not answer directly, "Why don't you investigate, meditate, and find out for yourself?" The son meditates for a while, gets an idea, and goes to his father for verification. "Reality is matter—the stuff of which my body is made, the stuff of the food that I eat. My body is *annamaya kosha*--a sheath made of *anna*—the food I eat." The father approves. "Yes," he says, "but meditate some more." The boy goes away, meditates, and after a while, based on his experience no doubt, has another idea. "Reality is the world of *prana*, vital energy, the container of energy that I feel—vitality; my body has a second sheath of vital energies—*pranamaya* kosha," he declares to his father this time. The father approves but encourages him to research and meditate some more. The boy does what he is told; soon he has another idea. "Reality is mind, the vehicle with which we think and explore meaning; my body has a third sheath made of mind—*manomaya kosha*, father." Father says, "Yes, but go deeper." The son is perseverant. This time he meditates and meditates and finally discovers intuition with shiver in his spine and runs to his father. "Father, father. I found it, I

1

found it. Reality is a world made of stuff of our intuition from which our sciences come, the context of what matter does, what vital energy movements are all about, even the contexts of our thinking; they are *Vi-gnyana*, the context of *gnyana*– knowledge; they give us laws and values to live by; my body has a fourth kosha, *vignanamaya kosha*, sheath made of the highest contexts of feeling and thinking." He is talking about the archetypes of course, a concept that the philosopher Plato introduced millennia later. A smile breaks on his father's face. But he says. "Good. But go deeper still my son." No matter, as the son is really motivated now, and he meditates again and discovers the oneness of everything, that reality is one and only, with joy that knows no boundaries. His being fills with joy and a certainty comes to him. This is it. The final sheath is anandamaya kosha—the sheath of limitless joy— *ananda*. He does not go back to his father any more, as he realises that there is no need to confirm this time.

What do you think of this story and what it is telling us? A man, a foreigner, on the street is in a hurry; he is late for an appointment but he has no watch to check how late. So, he asks a passer-by in his broken English,

"What's time?"

The passer-by is puzzled by the question,

"I don't know. Never thought about it. Isn't it a question of philosophy and for philosophers?"

Ok, you may feel the same way about questions on reality. I am aware you are not a researcher of reality, nor are you a philosopher, your knowledge about what you are, and that you have only one body, are all derived knowledge that you pick up in schools and colleges and perhaps on the Internet. Your main asset is that you are interested to know; you have looked at some of the knowledge of reality that is around, and that does not satisfy you. You are hungry for meaning and purpose in your life; but, the existing knowledge, (much of it anyway,) says there is none. You don't want to believe that.

You may have noticed one thing that should surprise a modern person. This lad's research technique is mainly meditative. Is it possible to discover the nature of reality through mere meditation? Well, let's elaborate a little. Meditation, suitably done with a burning question in mind, can give rise to creative experiences culminating with deep original insights.

Can one take knowledge gained by experience seriously? You wonder. Today, more and more scientists talk about evidence-based science, only objective evidence collected through our sophisticated machines is reliable.

I have got news for you. Quantum physics unequivocally says, *reality comes to us only as experience.* There is only potentiality outside of our experience. There is no objective reality sitting out there independent of our experience. Go figure.

So those guys who wrote the Upanishads, already knew something which we have discovered only after seven thousand years, including four hundred years of modern science. In India, they call guys like the writers of Upanishad *rishi,* seer of Truth.

Yes, Truth can be discovered through our experiences of intuition and creative insights. Even today's scientists— Einstein, Heisenberg, Schroedinger—they all did that. The interesting question is, why is there so much consorted effort to suppress this fact? When you investigate this question, the answer is revealing.

Why? *Because there is no way to make room for experience within the current scientific mainstream worldview.*

I was reading a book on neuroscience by a brain scientist trying to understand the brain from the point of view of conventional mainstream science. I thought the way he deals with quantum physics is cute. You know quantum physics is stubborn about one thing, and that is *experience*. Objects manifest only when we experience them; or else they are only potentialities. In view of quantum physics' stubborn conclusion, experience cannot be denied to the human being, this neuroscientist agrees. So according to him, human beings are mechanical and robotic, but they are no ordinary robots; they are robots with experience. He coins a new word, p-robot for a human being, where *p* stands for philosophical. Experience, yes, but our experiences have no causal consequences, no ability to change anything in the world; it is only ornamental, only a matter of philosophy, he maintains.

Why you ask, why such attempts at denigration of human experience, while human experience deployed and embodiedis what has given us civilization? An experience has two poles—subject and object. The subject or self is the experiencer (such as the "I" who is reading this page) and the object is what is experienced. In the case of this page the subject is experiencing meaning, the object of experience is meaning. The current mainstream worldview is called scientific materialism—the idea that every phenomenon is a material phenomenon caused by material interaction between material objects moving in space and time. According to this view, your brain is made of elementary particles of matter making atoms, making molecules, making neurons, making the brain... objects all the way. You cannot get a subject out of objects; they are two different categories of logic. Nor can you get meaning. Naturally, materialists try to denigrate the subject part of reality and objects of experience like meaning.

As I have shown long ago, (three decades now,) quantum physics, when properly interpreted without creating paradoxes, leads to an understanding of how the brain is more than a conglomerate of neurons because it has a subject or self; and also, how it acquires the self, how it embodies meaning, and how experiences happen in conjunction with the brain.

I will take the risk of immodesty. When Einstein in 1915 discovered a complicated theory of gravity called general relativity that used the unfamiliar math of tensor calculus and non-Euclidean geometry, rumour had it that for quite a while only twelve scientists in the whole world could understand the theory. Today, the list of establishment physicists who dare to understand quantum physics could be even less. It is not their IQ but their belief system that is the problem! To paraphrase Jesus, it is easier for a camel to go through the eye of a needle than for a scientific materialist to understand the meaning of quantum physics.

And yet, those *rishis* of the Upanishads some seven thousand years ago understood the importance of experience and experiential investigation in consciousness research. Today, our sociologists, mainly of materialist vintage try to denigrate ancient people as "mythical," and not at par with our superior rational minds. Huh?

So dear reader, suspend your prejudices and disbeliefs for the while that will take you to read the book. And I hope the following changes will happen in your understanding of reality:

1. Reality comes to us as a layered cake, each layer acts like a sheath of ignorance only until you understand it.

2. The first layer comes to you as one of external experience, and you do have a physical body with fixity—a structure—that perhaps is the biggest camouflage of reality one ever saw. However, an unbiased examination of quantum physics is all you need to see through the camouflage.

3. The other layers are experienced inside of you. You have bodies in each of these layers too, but these four bodies are subtle. The bodies in the second and third layers—the vital layer that gives us the experience of feeling and the mental layer that gives us the experience of thinking—have functional fixity in the form of frequently invoked memory. Beyond this it gets ever more subtle.

4. In quantum science, we call the stuff of intuition supramental archetypes. We cannot make direct memory of the supramental archetypes; so, we make archetypal memory and a functional archetypal body—traditions call it soul—using thoughts and feelings. But the soul thus made is really just a "higher mental-vital body." The last body—called the quantum self beyond our ego, (traditionally called spirit)—has no fixity; it is the doorway to oneness. Quantum science will help you navigate the darkness of these layers and bodies into more and more light.

5. As you taste your cake layer by layer, the darkness of your ignorance gives way to light of wisdom. With wisdom, the joy (the Sanskrit word is *ananda*) of the taste becomes your permanent fixture to behold. Ideally, eating would consist of incorporating the wisdom in your body and/or brain. But even conceptual understanding would entail a partial clearance of the darkness.

6. As you are undoubtedly aware, there are human beings aplenty around you, who do behave like P-robots, the neuroscientist is not entirely wrong. As you penetrate the cake layer by layer, a surprise awaits you. You will discover new creative freedom and an expansion of consciousness with increasing ability to include others. The more your consciousness expands, the happier you become, and the more you are capable of service to the needy. In this way the world can transform with you.

7. Concomitantly, the more you use your creative freedom in this fashion, the further you will penetrate the cake of reality with increasing happiness and intelligence.

And finally, appreciate the following lines from the Upanishad. Recite them often, aloud or silent, either way. They are empowering: First in Sanskrit,

Asato ma sat gamaya
Tamaso ma jyotir gamaya
Mrityur ma amritam gamaya

In English:

Take me from untruth to truth,
From darkness to light
From suffering (death) to happiness (immortality).

II
The Material Realism/Monistic Idealism Debate

The Upanishadic story that I started the book with throws you right in the midst of a theoretical approach to reality that I call monistic Idealism. Idealism means consciousness and its ideas or potentialities are the primary components of reality. So, why use the adjective monistic?

Undeniably, our experiences fall into two distinct categories: 1) External and public and 2) Internal and private. Many people are still moved by this undeniable difference between our two sets of experiences to suggest what is called the metaphysic of dualism: there are two dual components of reality; one is matter moving in space and time, the external component of reality; the dual internal partner is traditionally referred to as non-material mind and more recently as psyche. Dualism is matter-mind or matter-psyche dualism.

Well, but what mediates the interaction between the dual partners of reality? Before quantum physics came along, nobody had any idea of such a mediator. An alternative idea called psychophysical parallelism made some sense: the worlds of mind and matter are parallel worlds. This idea too has a severe critique: in view of the fact that everything changes, what maintains the parallelism?

Then about 7000 years ago, the rishis of the Upanishads discovered the concept of a monistic reality: reality is *Brahman*—represented by three qualifications, *sat*—existence, *chit*, subject-object conscious awareness, and *ananda*—joy. *Sarvam Kalyidam Brahman*—all is Brahman, declared the rishis based on their creative insight. Brahman contains both matter and mind. There is no dualism. In modern lingo, Brahman translates as consciousness. Consciousness is the ground of all being, both matter and mind. This defines the theory of monistic idealism.

Scientific materialism is the opposite theory of reality. There is still another rational way to solve the dualism problem: suppose mind or psyche is epiphenomena, secondary phenomena of matter itself. Just as water gives us the experience of wetness, brain matter gives us the experience of the internal mind or psyche, which has no separate and independent existence. Matter is everything, it is the ground of all being; material monism aka scientific materialism. (I hope you see that there is still persistent dualism between experiencer and the brain although this is a legitimate matter-psyche monism!)

This theory, too, has a lineage that goes back to Greek philosopher Democritus who lived some three thousand years back. In India, a similar materialist theory exists in the writings of Charvaka.

Two different theories of reality, each suggesting a life style radically different from the other. Materialism is easier to live; the Greek philosopher Epicurus summarized its dictum long ago: eat, drink, and be merry. In India Charvaka summarized the life style of materialism this way:

Yabat jibet, sukham jibet
Rinam kritya, Ghritam pibet

Meaning in English:

So long as you live, live pleasure-fully
Borrowing money and drinking *ghee*.

Ghee is clarified butter; like olive oil it is healthy yet tasty fat. Charvaka is suggesting what we today call a Mediterranean diet... with borrowed money! Smárt, huh?

Modern materialists are even smarter. They make sure that the lifestyle eliminates all possibilities to stray away from the attachment to physicality. They keep you from experiencing the third layer of the cake—the mind of meaning—by encouraging information processing—information is old meaning already in the brain's computer. When you engage with your cell phones, laptops and social media, the meanings you gather for avoiding boredom are other people's old meanings.

They also want you to eliminate the second layer of the cake from your experience. In a comic strip called *Pearls before swine*, in the first frame, one of the comic characters Rat says to another, Goat, "I am finally happy."

"You are?" asks Goat taking the bait.

"Yes," Rat declares in the second frame, "Even with all the pain and suffering in the world, I've finally found a way to be truly happy.

"I have lost the ability to feel," he finishes his thought in the third frame.

In the last frame, Goat comments to Pig, "Sociopaths have it so easy."

Idealism sees the desired human lifestyle differently. Reality has these higher layers and exploring them is increasingly happiness producing. Why be stuck with the ignorance that you are just the material body. Isn't it true that material body gives pleasure as well as pain and suffering? Due to illness, due to old age, and then there is always death. *Why not explore the higher layers of reality, subtle they may be, but there is energy and passion there, there is meaning that mind brings, and purpose lies with the exploration of the archetypes like abundance and love, and the self.*

Sounds pretty good when put this way. But underneath, there is an unpleasant message: leave the pleasure of the flesh behind. Also, it is hard to believe that suffering of disease, old age, and death goes away just because you have changed your perspective.

What does history say about the influence of these theories on people's lives? History is muddled because something happened to the idealist theory when it was popularized for the masses in a way it could compete with the materialist life style's pleasureful and permissive offerings. I am talking about religion.

How can you entice a person to give up tangible pleasure of the flesh with only the promise of intangible "something" that you call happiness or joy—*ananda*? Can we really escape suffering of ailments and old age and death by the pursuit of wisdom? If people ask, show me, you yourself will find reluctance in giving up pleasure of the flesh (for today's people, additionally pleasure of the cell phone and social media!). It is much easier to talk about idealism than pursue it in your life.

But if you do believe in idealism and you do think that there is a sellable marketable product here if only you can come up with the right campaign, then Bingo. You come up with the idea of sin. It is sinful to partake in pleasure.

But that won't jive with the all-encompassing oneness idea of reality. Make a compromise. Replace the concept of unity consciousness; replace the concept of archetypes which in popular mind, stands as individual gods to explore and worship by *one* monotheistic God, omniscient and omnipotent. Your model of God almighty is King of kings. Just as early kings dispose of justice to their subjects, the King of kings delivers justice to the sinner at the moment of death—on the judgment day. If you commit sin during life you pay for it in death, you are sent to eternal hell of fire and brimstone. The most successful religion of the world—the Judeo-Christian religions--sell their product this way.

In actuality, sophisticates explain, religions are not entirely lying. The fire of hell is the fire of unfulfillable desires that go with you as part of your character when you die. Heaven and hell are not separate places; they don't have to be.

A rabbi goes to the after world upon death and immediately he thinks of finding his long-deceased beloved teacher, another rabbi. When he finds him, he is surprised. The rabbi is sitting in his usual chair reading Kabala, the book of Jewish wisdom tradition like the Indian Upanishads, but lo! There is a beautiful naked woman on his bed, moaning and groaning with desire. He grins devilishly and winks at his teacher. "Rabbi, is that your reward for all the good deeds you did during your life?" he asks pointing to the woman in heat. The rabbi looks up and says, "No son. You got it all wrong. *I* am her punishment, her hell."

The same idea is conveyed in the following story from the Orient. Heaven and hell both consist of banquet halls with comfortable chairs to sit on, with like-minded others around big banquet size tables laid out with sumptuous food. However, the knives forks, and spoons, are all big, the size of the entire length of the table. People live in hell when each vainly tries to feed himself or herself with those oversized cutlery; they live in heaven when each occupant feeds the person sitting on the opposite side of the table.

In this manner there is even a mystical way to rationalize the concept of hell with another intriguing but scientific idea: survival after death. The Upanishads go even further: they suggest the price you pay for committing sin is reincarnation with bad habit patterns (karma) that leadto suffering.

The net offshoot of the concept of sin is that now idealism can be marketed by instilling fear of hell or fear of bad karma. Fear works much better as a marketing tool than vague promises of happiness of exploring meaning and purpose.

In this way, idealism in the compromised form of religion has been much more popular throughout human history. Until modern science came along with the promise of verification of theories by experimental data. This single idea challenged the concept of hell and a doler of punishment image of God, so much so that religions lost their competitive advantage over materialism.

On top of this, materialism became scientific with tons of verification of its main ideas: Committing Sin, the propensity of acting under the influence of negative emotions like anger, lust, and domination of others are built into the human brain just as pleasure seeking is. As is the tendency of selfishness and egotism, these traits are also built into the brain. We are the way we are, a product of nature--genetic inheritance--or nurture—sociocultural conditioning.

The scientists of materialist science conclude: We are what we are. We cannot change by following purposive ideals—those archetypes—because they don't exist, but so what? The human condition isn't so bad and we can make it better through ever new technology.

And scientific materialists have delivered. Today, there is unprecedented material prosperity in the world, never mind that it is not equitably shared wealth among all people. Technology has minimized suffering, almost eliminated even the suffering of boredom. Today's human child, when he or she is bored just has to pick up the cell phone, where lies the promise of infinite supply of information to occupy oneself, never mind that it has a dumbing down effect on the child.

But idealists do not see things in the way of materialists; they complain. Not only about the side effects of materialist products but about the theoretical incompleteness of scientific materialism in its ability to describe the complete human being.

And yet most of these modern idealists are rational thinkers, they are pragmatists; their pragmatism demands that their theories never challenge the fundamental premise of scientific materialism—everything is matter. They play with ideas like holism—the whole is greater than the parts. Or complexity theory: when things get sufficiently complex, new things like life or consciousness can emerge from matter itself (emergentism).

One exception is transpersonal psychology founded by Abraham Maslow, Stan Grof and others. Transpersonal psychology tries to adapt monistic idealism by expanding cognitive/behavioural materialist psychology with the concept of a transpersonal self that brings unity consciousness of the Upanishads into a manifest being.

There are two pathways in which transpersonal psychology is developing. One is to avoid challenging scientific materialism and yet boldly by-pass it to make room for the transpersonal self. This is the path that the philosopher Ken Wilber has charted.

In Wilber's four-quadrant model, reality is divided into four quadrants (fig. 1). The two quadrants on the right are the objective side of things, the "it" and "its" view of things: leave them to the scientists. The two quadrants on the left are the subjective side, the point of view of *I* (top quadrant) and *we* (bottom quadrant). They belong to transpersonal psychology.

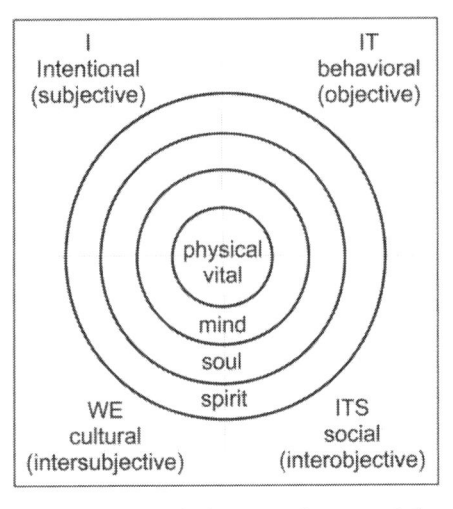

Fig. 1: Wilber's four-quadrant model

Unfortunately, although "I" can be treated both in its ego and transpersonal aspect, but its connection to the brain is left out. So, it is a disembodied *I* that clearly smacks of dualism. Wilber claims that the dualism clears up only when you are enlightened.

The other pathway of transpersonal psychology is to try to put the original Upanishadic monistic idealism in psychological garb and seek a scientific solution to its unresolved very scientific questions. Among them, *How does consciousness expresses itself in the brain?* is the paramount one.

Abraham Maslow, the founder of transpersonal psychology along with Stan Grof, believed that ultimately science must explain "everything that is the case." There is so much experiential evidence of spiritual transformation of people achieving various stations of increasing role played by the transpersonal self that it is entirely non-scientific to throw the evidence away, says Grof based on the vast new data he himself has collected.

The scientific materialists got too hasty to close the door of science to look for a science of consciousness. From the beginning, even when materialists tried to compromise quantum physics' message trying to fit it within the straightjacket of scientific materialism (that interpretation is called the Copenhagen Interpretation orchestrated by the famous Niels Bohr), one thing was always clear. It is impossible to eliminate the role of the subject entirely from quantum physics.

Most materialists refused to take that as a hint that quantum physics is the right vehicle that consciousness rides to manifest itself in the brain. I took the hint and the reward is a complete science of consciousness and its experiences—how unity consciousness splits itself into a subject in the brain and objects of experiences. I will summarize the main results in the next section. The rest of the book is devoted to the details.

III
Quantum Science

In 2004, I got my one-year of name and fame when I appeared as a protagonist of quantum physics in the popular feature film *What the Bleep Do We Know?* In that I said the famous one liner, "Quantum physics is the physics of possibilities." Indeed so. In my paradox-free formulation of quantum physics, quantum objects *are* waves of possibility for consciousness to choose from, only that it is not the choice of the individual ego but that of a Oneness consciousness that lies unconscious in us. As this Oneness consciousness chooses, it identifies itself with the brain through whose "eyes" it is looking at the object of concern.

If these lines seem slightly obtuse, don't be dismayed. There will be more details in the next chapter where I promise to hold your hands all the way to help you penetrate all the illusions that the first layer of our reality cake, the material world, creates.

It had been a difficult journey for me myself, that began in 1973, with what creativity theorists call a crystallization experience. Until then, I was an unabashed believer of scientific materialism. I was successful in my academic pursuit, a professor of physics at the University of Oregon (before it became a football university), a rising star in my field of expertise. But I was not happy. I had no congruence in my life.

In 1973, I was invited to an American Physical Society meeting to give a talk, which was considered quite prestigious. I gave my spiel and felt it went quite well, but that feeling did not last long. As other speakers presented, I felt they were doing a much better job and naturally getting more attention, and I was jealous. The jealousy only increased during the course of the day. In the evening, I went to a party in honour of the speakers, and now I was getting jealous because others were getting more attention than my suave self from the women at the party. At 1 a.m., I noticed that I had consumed an entire packet of antacids, and I still had heartburn! I felt disgusted and went outside. The party was being held at a place called Asilomar on Monterey Bay. As I stood on the terrace, ocean air hit my face, and a thought came to me out of nowhere: *Why do I live this way?* And at that very moment I knew. I knew I didn't have to live this schizophrenia between my life and how I made my livelihood. I could integrate. I could do happy physics. I could become whole again.

And then a series of coincidences took place which Carl Jung would call synchronicities. I marry an American woman who is eager to participate in my trials and tribulations in searching for happy physics to engage in. A co-ed hears metalk about the possibility of finding happy physics and literally guides me to purchase a newly published book called *The Tao of Physics*. Somebody else gifts a book to me co-authored by the physicist Fred Alan Wolf where he creates the slogan based on a new interpretation of quantum physics by John von Neumann, *we create our own reality*. Do we really? How? My curiosity was perked. I had found the vehicle for happy physics. It was going to be quantum physics.

Von Neumann and Wolf had boldly introduced consciousness into physics—observer's consciousness chooses manifest reality from all the possibilities that a quantum object represents. But their view is riddled with paradoxes that they could not solve.

I intuited that understanding the nature of consciousness was the key here. However, the experts who were supposed to know, psychologists and neuroscientists, I found out, did not know much. All were groping in the darkness looking for an understanding of what consciousness is.

One night I saw a dream. My father, who while alive was sort of a small-scale spiritual guru to a few disciples, appeared in the dream with a snake in his hand. Then he threw the snake at me and as I caught it, he disappeared. A friend interpreted the dream as transformational, an invitation for me to transform. Transformation? What does that mean?

I soon found out. Transformation requires enlightenment; an experience that Zen Buddhists talk about a lot. I becamean avid student of Zen and pondered quite a few Zen koans, paradoxical statements, pondering over which you achieve sudden enlightenment.

I could see many parallels between Zen and quantum physics. For example, the idea of sudden enlightenment was much like a quantum leap that atomic electrons take when they shift orbits. They don't go through the intervening space between the two orbits. Similarly, enlightenment is not the product of step-by-step rational thinking. *Was enlightenment a quantum leap from our ego to the transpersonal self that transpersonal psychologists propose? Does that leap produce transformation?*

I joined a meditation group, followers of Swami Muktananda who gave something called s*haktipot* to his disciples. *Shakti* is a Sanskrit word that translates as energy; this guy waves feathers and that generates Shakti in his disciples, his disciples assured me. But how can that be? It violates the energy conservation law: energy cannot be created.

Then Muktananda got caught in a sexual scandal causing me much uneasiness. *How can an enlightened person who has known ananda be tempted by mere sexual pleasure?*

I met a couple of new age gurus who claimed enlightenment. But on closer examination, their enlightenment seemed a lot connected with their adventures with LSD. *Can enlightenment be effected by drugs like LSD?*

My research into consciousness led to many questions and few answers. In particular no answer came for the question of quantum physics that Von Neumann and Wolf raised: *Does my consciousness choose actuality from quantum possibilities and create reality and not paradox?*

I will give details in chapters 2 and 3, but in 1985 I finally had my answer. Yes, my intuition was correct; quantum physics leads us to a science of consciousness and gives us an explanation of how the brain becomes the subject pole of our experience of the world. That was the beginning. It took many years to research all the facets of the great varieties of human experience. Finally, here it is, a complete quantum science of human experience.

Chapter 2

The First Layer of the Reality cake: The Physical World and Quantum Physics that Governs it

I
An Introduction to Quantum Physics

The first layer of the cake of reality, the first sheath is the physical world and matter that constitutes the substance of the physical world, is made of stuff that can be reduced to smaller stuff. In other words, the macro matter around us, tables, chairs, buildings, all can be broken down into more basic ingredients of matter. The surprise was that after a while of this breaking down to smaller bits, we come across some base level building blocks—elementary particles. Matter cannot be broken down any further.

We express this formally by saying that matter consists of a simple hierarchy of stuff: elementary particles make atoms, atoms make molecule, molecules make bulk matter (fig. 2). Simple hierarchy means it is causally one-way up; upward causation. All cause exists as interaction between elementary particles. Any causes we attribute for convenience to the higher levels of the hierarchy are just that, for convenience; we can say force between atoms, because it is convenient to think like that. But underneath, we always remember that such atomic forces are really the consequence of interactions between the elementary particles, electrons, quarks and such.

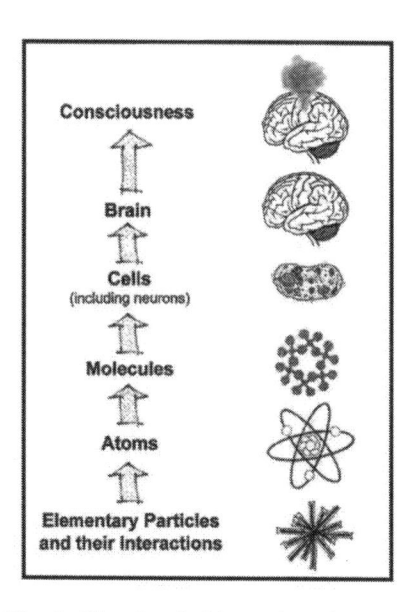

Fig. 2: The simple hierarchy of matter

Simple hierarchy! Elementary particles interact and that affects all the upper layers. But the upper layers cannot affect the workings of the elementary particles. Like how you conceptualize a patriarchy, father knows best.

And then there is the concept of energy. When you run, you have kinetic energy. A boulder sitting on a hill has potential energy; it is released as kinetic energy if you push the boulder off the hill. There are many forms of potential energy.

So, energy can be converted from one form into another. When two objects interact, they exchange energy via signals that take energy from one body to the other very locally, a little distance at a time obeying a speed limit—the speed of light. There is a law called law of conservation of energy: in all such conversion or energy exchange, the total energy of the world always remains a constant.

For a long time, physicists thought that energy surely can be broken down indefinitely, they can be exchanged in any denominations, however small. Quantum physics was glimpsed when a physicist named Max Planck discovered that like matter, energy, too could be broken down only so far. Planck gave a special name to the elementary particle of energy—quantum, plural quanta.

In retrospect, this was a momentous discovery; and yet, nobody understood the importance of it until a patent clerk named Albert Einstein figured out something that created a huge puzzle that even you the non-scientist can appreciate.

Young Albert's reasoning was simple enough; the reason all the erudite physicists of the day could not think it is probably because they did not take Planck's idea seriously enough to apply it for other situations. Planck was working with radiant energy; Einstein was working with visible light. Einstein just noted heat radiation is also a kind of light—infrared, invisible, but like visible light it also consists of electromagnetic waves.

Now do you see? A quantum of radiant energy is an elementary particle of light; we call it a photon nowadays. Particles are very localized, even when they move, they describe a trajectory staying in one place at a time. But light is also wave, a property known since the days of Newton. This is a puzzle when you think about it.

Throw a pebble in a pond creating a water wave and you will see the point. The water waves spread out; the crest lines embrace many different places at the same time. So, the puzzle: *how can the same object be both at one place and spread out all over at the same time, how can it be both a particle and a wave?*

But you cannot doubt experimental data: matter and energy both are wave and particle. It took people a long time to get the significance of the puzzle; in truth, some scientists still don't see the significance. They always say, nobody understands quantum physics! As if that is a virtue.

In the eighties, Californians coined a very appropriate phrase for this kind of behaviour—in box thinking. Thinking while putting oneself inside an invisible box of beliefs. Another way of saying it would be thinking by wearing a straitjacket. Yes, appropriate for a mad person, but physicists are supposed to be sane, brilliant, people of 150 IQ and better!

Belief systems do strange things to people. Scientific materialism is such a belief system. You know modern science grew out of a feud with Christianity and many scientists are still fighting it. Religions generally believe, and Christianity is no exception, that beyond this immanent world of space and time and matter, there is another world that transcends it, the abode of God, an all-powerful King of kings. Religions call God's causal power "downward" causation, consistent with the picture of God in heaven "up" there.

Of course, scientists cannot believe such simplistic nonsense about God and God's power! Where is the evidence? Haven't we gone to the outer space where supposedly heaven exists? Haven't we demonstrated that so-called heavenly objects—the moon, the planets, and the stars, all are subject to the same earthly laws ever since Newton? Haven't we demonstrated time and time again that all phenomena can be understood as the result of material interactions alone?

Face it, scientists have been saying to religions: outer space is just part of ordinary space which is all the space there is, all the space in which objects—material objects--can exist. There is no evidence for dualism: a transcendent dual world of heaven of God, or downward causation. How would downward causation work except through exchange of signals carrying energy? But lo! Remember that the energy of the material world is conserved. No energy has ever been found to disappear from this world to God's world if you are thinking of God living in a dual world. A science based on scientific materialism is all we need to understand reality.

Except this pesky little thing, this little wave-particle quantum paradox.

II
Particles and Waves

I hope you enjoyed going through the historical lane of quantum physics. Now let's get into some nitty-gritty about some of the concepts, some necessary details, necessary for deep understanding and further exploration. Let's also enumerate all the different aspects of quantum science that we have touched upon and that is giving us a new conceptual lens to look at the world, a quantum worldview.

I think both earlier worldviews—spiritual/religious idealism and Scientific materialism take our power away. One ism says power lies with God—downward causation; the other ism says, power lies with the material elementary particles—upward causation. The quantum worldview, I declare is different: it empowers *you* as well. How so?

Particles and Waves

Isaac Newton introduced the concept of particles and the laws of their movement. Particles are localized objects; their ideal picture is that of billiard balls. They have a natural motion: either the state of rest or the state of uniform motion of constant speed and direction. Natural motion is relative; you cannot tell if an object is in a state of rest or in uniform motion at constant velocity. Try if you can tell from inside a moving train in uniform motion if it is moving or not without looking outside. You can't.

To change the state of uniform natural motion, you have to exert a force. Newton's laws tell us mathematically how forces operate to change an object's natural motion. That's it. The rest of physics is to learn the nature of all the different material forces and the math for solving different situations.

There is also the concept of energy. If the object is moving, the object obviously has the capacity to get things going; we call this capacity for doing work kinetic energy. If an object is held together by forces but not moving, obviously its capacity for doing work is a potential capacity--potential energy. So instead of force, we can say, there is potential energy.

Why bring up energy? Energy can be brought from one place to another by waves, that's why. Look at a wind-driven water wave in the ocean and how it brings all that energy to the shore. Wave energy helps us communicate.

How do we depict a water wave? Look closely. A water wave is a travelling disturbance of the water. We can quantify the disturbance by the amount of displacement of the water molecules from the undisturbed level of water. When we plot the disturbance quantified this way, we get fig. 3.

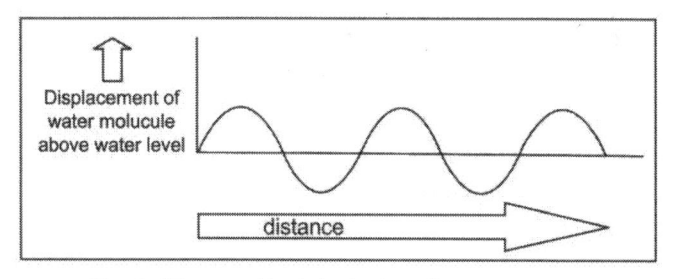

Fig. 3: The graphical depiction of a water wave

Couple of things about the wave is worth mentioning: 1) Wavelength is the distance the wave travels before repeating itself; simple the length of a wave, traversing which the waves comes back to the same phase. 2) The number of wave cycles per second is called frequency.

In my childhood, I used to throw pebble in water andwatched the concentric expanding crest circles for hours. My kid brother used to tease me. "What are waves good for?"

One day I spontaneously responded with a poem:

Waves teach us how to listen

And how to watch;

Waves can teach us love.

Newtonian waves—water waves, sound waves, light waves—they cannot teach us about love. But some quantum waves can. You will see. How I anticipated that at a young age I don't know.

Waves and Particles in Quantum Physics

Quantum equation of movement is a wave equation—its solution is a wave. For sure it is a peculiar wave. For the water wave, it is the disturbance of the water from level that propagates (fig. 3). For a quantum wave what propagates is what is called a wave function related to the probability of finding the object as particle when we did measure the wave. Think of the wave function as a possibility function, a quantification of the probability for the various possibilities (Fig. 4a)

Let's take you through a simple thought experiment. To begin, we release a single electron virtually at rest from an electron shooter into the middle of a room. According to the quantum equation, the wave now propagates growing bigger and bigger as expanding spheres of crest and soon is all over the room. To check if the electron is really all over the room, we set up a three-dimensional grid of Geiger counters (electron detectors) all over the room.

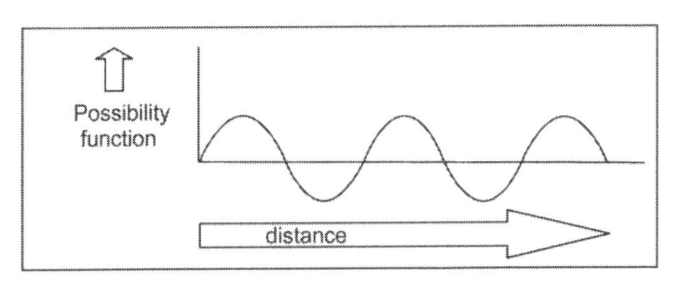

fig. 4 (a): The graphical depiction of a quantum possibility wave;

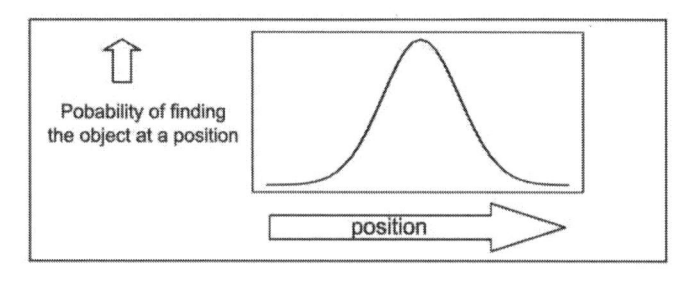

fig. 4 (b): quantum probability distribution

First of all, will all the Geiger counters tick? No, measurement converts the wave into a particle; so only one Geiger counter ticks. How do we know then that the electron wave did really expand all over the room? We have to repeat the experiment with an identical electron released in identical condition many times. If we do that, indeed the electron does show up in all the different places in the room with various probabilities. If we plot the probability of finding the electron at a given position against position, we get a bell curve, the standard probability distribution curve that the quantum equation predicts will happen (fig. 4b).

In this way, the wisdom dawns: the electron's wave is a possibility wave. A possibility wave cannot reside in space and time; its domain is the domain of potentiality—outside of space and time. When we measure, the wave collapses—transforms from a wave to a particle--it discontinuously appears in space and time, localized particle-like. But this is no Newtonian particle, always appearing in the place determined by material forces. There is no way to predict where the electron-particle will appear in a given experiment. The cause is not a material cause; the cause comes from the domain of potentiality in the form of downward causation—a choice from among the various possible positions.

Three scientists, Einstein, Podolsky, and Rosen showed that the domain of potentiality is also a domain of potential oneness. Any two or more objects can come close, interact via material forces and become correlated (nowadays we also say entangled) and achieve oneness—ability of instant communication among one another whatever their distance from one another. This property is technically called nonlocality (fig. 5). See next chapter for further elaboration.

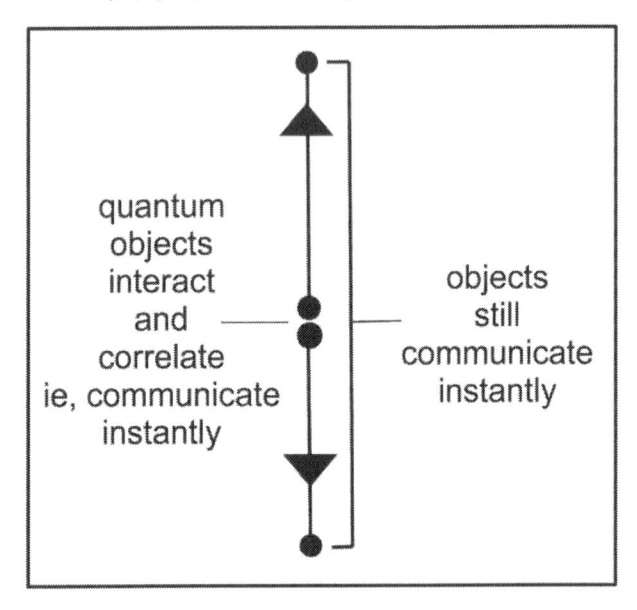

```
quantum
objects
interact                    objects
and          ————           still
correlate                   communicate
ie, communicate             instantly
instantly
```

fig. 5: The EPR paradox: instant communication (nonlocality) between correlated quantum objects

Since in any experiment, what actualizes is not only a manifest object but also an observer's conscious self that experiences the object, we conclude that the oneness is consciousness—the measurement splits the oneness into a duality of subject and object. Downward causation is conscious choice, *not* a force, *not* a quantum force field as some researchers theorize.

The Double-slit Experiment

Now let's talk about an actual laboratory experiment where an electron wave goes through a double-slitted screen, splits into two waves—one at each slit—the waves add, an effect technically called interference—and the electron's net wave is detected on a photographic plate or a fluorescent screen where you can see the electron collapsing at a point of the screen. It collapses as a particle should, as a dot at one place on the photographic plate

In the olden days they did the experiment shooting electrons from an electron gun in a bunch at once causing a lot of confusion. Then a graduate student wanted to see what happens in such experiments if we use a slow electron gun that shoots the electron one first, and after a while another, and on and on; so, on the average only one electron at a time is subjected to the experiment. But the young fellow had a date. Since the experiment would take a long time, the fellow went on his date and forgot about his pending experiment. When he remembered after a couple of days and checked on the progress of his experiment, he was amazed. The result of all the electrons each individually collapsing on the plate was a wave pattern indeed. For the double slit arrangement, this means that even when one electron at a time passes through the two slits of the screen, we get wave behavior called the wave interference pattern (fig. 6a); only waves can produce it.

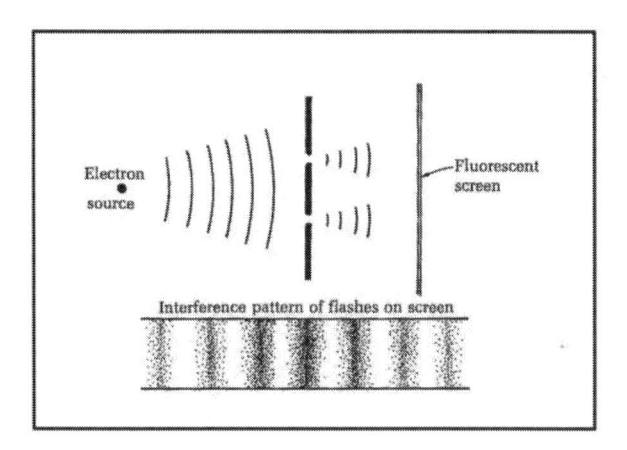

fig. 6 (a): The double slit arrangement and the interference pattern;

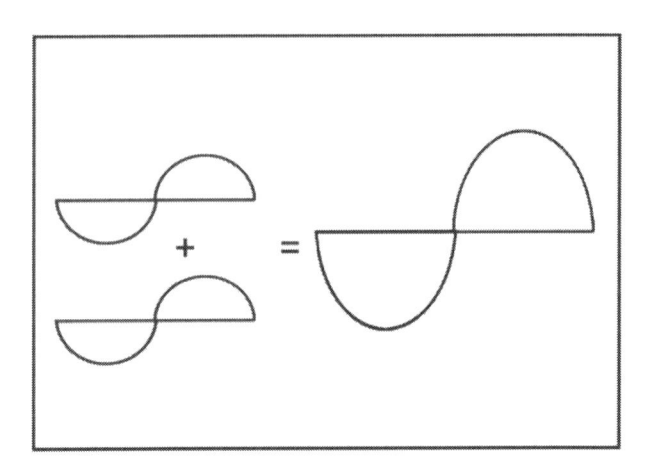

fig. 6 (b): when two waves arrive at a place in phase, they reinforce one another;

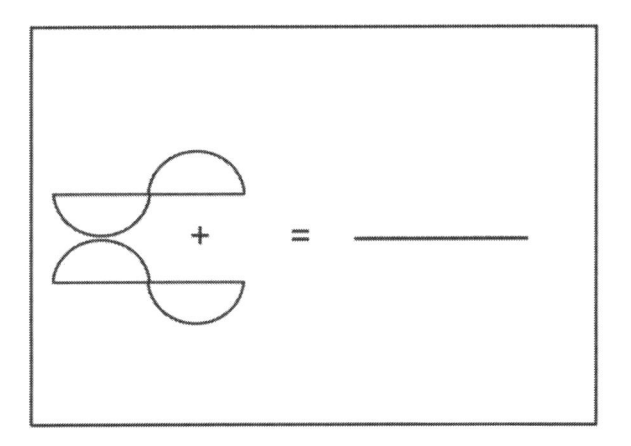

fig. 6 (c): when two waves arrive at a place out of phase, the cancel each other out

Let's see how wave addition produces an interference pattern. At each point of the plate, the waves from the two slits will travel a difference distance. If the distance each wave travels is an integer multiple of the wavelength of the waves, the waves will arrive at the place with the same phase, the same condition of the possibility function (fig. 6b) and add reinforcing each other. So, at these places, the probability of a particle appearing will be enhanced. But if one wave travels an integer multiple of wavelengths and the other travel an integer multiple plus one more half of a wavelength, they come to a place on the plate in opposite phases (fig. 6c) cancelling each other's effect. So, there is zero probability of particles appearing at these places.

In this way a double slit experiment always produces an interference pattern of alternate bright and dark fringes irrespective of whether we do the experiment with one electron at a time or a bunch of electrons all at the same time.

Conclusions:

1) Each electron interferes with itself; each electron is a wave. The waviness is not a bunch property.

2) At the photographic plate, the electron's wave collapses into a particle, but not a Newtonian particle, not always predictable to fall in front of either one or the other slit. So, seeing that the individually collapsed particles are hitting the plate in places not allowed to Newtonian particles, we can already conclude that the electron may be wave-like.

3) As in the thought experiment, only when we do the double slit experiment with many identical electrons, do we conclude that the electron is a wave of possibilities, going through both slits simultaneously in possibility, becoming two waves and interfering with each other.

The important point here is this. In quantum orthodoxy, people attempt to do away with the paradox of wave-particle duality by enunciating a complementarity principle: quantum objects are both wave and particle but you can measure only one aspect—the wave or the particle—of the object in a given experiment. This misleads you to think of wave-particle duality something like two sides of the same coin; you can see only one side in any given toss. This rationalization is wrong: the same double slit experiment does tell us that electrons are both particles and waves, except that *they are not both wave and particle in space and time.* Quantum objects are first of all, waves of possibility residing outside space and time; they become particles of actuality only when we measure them.

It turns out that the millennia old Chinese Taoist philosophy defined the concept of complementarity the same way: transcendent wave (*yin*) and immanent particle (*yang*).

Let's have more fun, tackle with an imaginary die-hard who insists that no object can go through two slits at the same time. They must be going through one slit or the other, maybe they deflect from the walls of a slit or something to explain why some of them appear as spots that are at odds from a Newtonian point of view. To prove the fellow wrong, you say, let's measure to see which slit the electron goes through. Let's imagine that we are seeing the electron throwing a flashlight on it, OK?

What happens when a strong flashlight is focused at one of the slits? Measuring the electron converts the electron wave into a particle and it now goes through the slit particle like and falls exactly on a spot behind the slit.

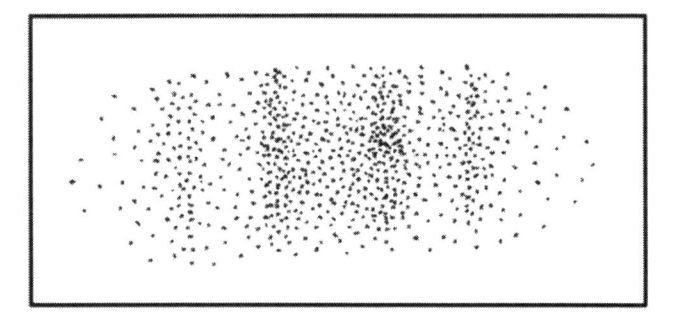

Fig. 7: If we look with a weak flashlight, some electrons will escape detection and become wavelike, so the interference pattern returns, albeit weak.

No more interference pattern! Indeed, this can be verified, not with flashlight but with more elaborate arrangements.

But you have even more fun with an imaginary flashlight whose intensity can be adjusted from strong to weak, to weaker, to off. What happens when we do the double slit experiment with a bunch of electrons passing the slits at once, except that we attempt to see with our imaginary flashlight which slit each electron passes through? As we make the flashlight progressively weaker and weaker, more and more electrons will escape detection, behave wavelike, and show some of the signs of the interference pattern (fig. 7). When the flashlight is off, the interference pattern will show up in full glory. Just for fun, I illustrate this progressive transition from electron being all-particle to them being all-wave as a cartoon, the man-girl sequence (fig. 8)

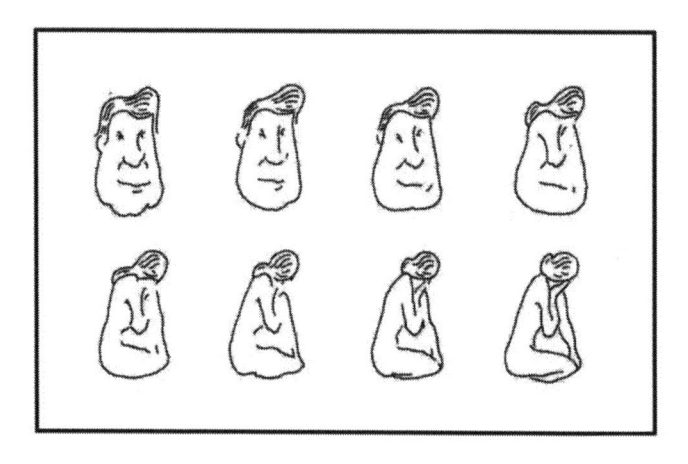

Fig. 8: The Man-girl sequence. After a cartoon by Gerald H. Fisher in 1967.

As far as I know, nobody has done this particular thought experiment to date. But I tell you this, nobody in their right mind will object to any of this depiction because quantum physics says this is the way it has to happen!

III
More Quantum Paradoxes

There are a couple of other paradoxes too to baffle the scientific materialist. All these paradoxes arise because we are using wrong lens to look at phenomena, wrong worldview. Solving them enlightens us enough to penetrate the physical sheath and scientific materialism.

One of these paradoxes is the famous Einstein-Podolsky-Rosen (abbreviated EPR) paradox mentioned already. What EPR proved was this: If two of those quantum objects interact, guess what? They achieve a state of correlation—a state in which they stay even when they move far away from each other and no longer interact. What is paradoxical about this state of correlation is that in this correlated state they can communicate instantly, no matter their distance. This violates the speed limit of the speed of light set by Einstein's own relativity theory that is sacrosanct.

Einstein was a Deist, a believer in a caretaker God who sets up the world in motion and never again interferes. In Hinduism, God has three aspects: Brahma—the initial creator with no further role; when the creation becomes stagnant Siva destroys the old and creates the new; in between Vishnu maintains the creation with interference, if necessary. So, Einstein's Deism is like Hinduism with Brahma alone, no Vishnu, and especially, no Shiva. Einstein did not like quantum possibility wave and all the mumbo-jumbo it creates. He was convinced that in view of EPR paradox, quantum physics is doomed to be a failure, at best incomplete.

Gradually, a few physicists began thinking out of the box. There was, after all another way of thinking that avoids the paradox. Except scientists have to give up one of their cherished beliefs. The quantum objects are waves, but they are waves of possibility residing in a separate domain of reality (call it the domain of potentiality). When they interact through material interaction, they acquire a field of oneness that mediates between them. When we measure, the waves collapse into separate particles instantaneously, nonlocally, through the agency of this field of oneness--nonlocal collapse, via downward causation. So EPR's idea does not have to be paradoxical!

But the beliefs one has to give up, they are stupendous. First of all, for hundreds of years, scientists have been talking about how important it is for people to recognize the difference between natural and supernatural and discard anything that smacks supernatural. Natural is one reality—space and time in which matter moves. Any religious talk of transcendent domain is talk about supernature, suspicious. Now to give that idea up and believe in a domain of potentiality outside space and time that can be experimentally discerned from space and time!

There is also a more technical aspect of all this. The belief that all communication must proceed through signals with a speed limit is called the principle of locality. Signal-less communication is nonlocal in clear violation of the locality principle.

As more conceptual clarity dawned, a few physicists became busy putting EPR in a measurable form so that an experiment can settle the issue: is there nonlocality—signal-less communication--or not? Einstein, elaborating on his idea that quantum physics is incomplete was in favour of hidden variables that dictated what states the correlated particle would manifest in; who needs communication?

Eventually, an avant-garde physicist named John Bell did find a measurable form that discredited hidden variables in favour of nonlocal communication.

Then in 1982, Alain Aspect and his collaborators in Paris demonstrated nonlocal communication between two correlated photons at a distance. Nowadays, even a graduate student given access to a physics lab can replicate Aspect's experimental demonstration.

I was watching all this from the side lines. I knew Aspect's experiment was a momentous event, but I still could not make the connection with consciousness. Perhaps I had lost faith in consciousness in the way mystics talk about it. It seemed to be all talk! Where is the demonstration?

In my childhood, I considered Indian version of spirituality; my parents represented it in their lives, in their own way. Yes! My father had a presence; I had felt it. It used to calm me down. My mother too was sincere in the family traditional offerings of *puja*s; how I loved those rituals. What turned me off were the contradictions my parents exhibited. I had an older brother who had a handicap—stammering. My father was often cruel and taunting to him. I could not rationalize my mother's left-handed behaviour to her daughters in law either. I was confused about the veracity of the spiritual traditions and religions and when the opportunity arose, I chose science to resolve my doubts about fundamental questions of life.

In a way it did! It shoved those questions under the rug as unimportant and instead kindled my passion for putting my mark in the scientific pursuit of knowledge. In other words, ambition; I developed a major dose of ambition.

That ambition ceased in 1973 with my crystallization experience and became replaced once again by the curiosity to know truth. In 1974, I had a tenured full professorship at a major public University in USA. If not now, when?

But as I looked into New Age spirituality, my enthusiasm abated and my doubts about the verity of spirituality came back. Right about that time, the physicist David Bohm suggested a realist's alternative to quantum physics and his theory was halfway mystical. For one thing, he did have a *domain of reality outside space and time that he called the Implicate Order.* In his theory implicate order becomes explicate order of material movement in space and time but it is no individual's conscious choice that does the transition. A nonlocal force determines the transition! So even nonlocality was included.

Like Einstein's God, David Bohm's God was also a Deist God, who like Brahma of Hinduism retires after setting the implicate and explicate orders in motion to go on perpetually determined by material forces plus that nonlocal force, a perpetual reminder of the implicate order of things. Where are *we* in all this schema, our freedom to choose, our creativity? David Bohm and his followers said, our free will and creativity are the play of chaos theory that was popular then. The idea is that things can be determined underneath, but superficially they look chaotic and creative because of the butterfly effect. A flapping of butterfly wings can change the weather, for example in a huge way, says chaos theory!

I was still confused, I still could not see my way out of scientific materialism, Bohm's theory notwithstanding.

One way to penetrate the prejudice of material supremacy and realist philosophy is to go back to the very beginning. Werner Heisenberg, the co-discoverer of quantum physics, also discovered the uncertainty principle obeyed by quantum objects: it is impossible to determine both the position and the velocity of a quantum object simultaneously with utmost accuracy. This translates into the further important piece of knowledge about quantum objects: we cannot determine exact trajectories of movement of quantum objects. This is uncertainty, indeterminacy.

Usually philosophers emphasize that the uncertainty principle raises the question of free will. The question is, whose free will? Electron's? But that is nonsense; electrons are just possibilities. Yes, uncertainty begets free will, and the free will must be about *our* free will, free will of the observer, of consciousness.

Indeed, in the seventies, the physicist Fred Alan Wolf, picking up on an earlier idea of mathematician John von Neumann, had created the slogan, *We create our own reality.*

But if we are forever stuck with base level human conditions that materialists have discovered, then do we really have free will to choose? Who cares about mundane choices like, *What flavour of ice cream do I want?* If that illusion of choice comes to us through determined chaos, does it really matter?

If our free will cannot lead to our transformation, what good is it? But I no longer had faith in spiritual transformation. And then I met Franklin.

IV
The Denouement: My discovery of the Science behind Experience

Back in the nineteen eighties, there was a time in my life when I was very unhappy and my unhappiness was affecting my marriage. In short, my wife and I fought a lot. Circumstances sent us both for a month to the ashram of an American enlightened mystic named Franklin Merrell Wolff situated in a small town named Lone Pine in California high up in the Sierra. Franklin was ninety-seven years old at the time. When I tried talking quantum physics with him, he refused. "It gives me headaches," he said. Since I liked him, and there was nothing else for me to do to spend the long summer afternoons (my wife was not available), I just sat with Franklin in his garden. Franklin napped while I vegetated. This went on for a while.

I was getting bored. There was nothing to serve the intellect. Then I started hearing people talk about a "delightful physicist" on the ground and became curious. "I'd like to meet him," I said and everybody laughed. Then I realized I was that physicist! A little internal checking showed that indeed I had been happy lately! My wife and I had found harmony.

What produced the transformation? I am convinced that it was the local proximity of Franklin that triggered in me a quantum nonlocal consciousness whose wholeness made me happy — induction effect. (Incidentally, as soon as wife and I left the campus, within a few minutes, we started fighting, right in the car proving that the effect was a temporary induction indeed!)

When I came back home, my faith in spiritual transformation was restored. Unfortunately, I became entangled in a personal melodrama almost immediately. When the clouds dissipated, I returned to the meaningful questions of quantum physics right away and decided to hear out another mystic Jiddu Krishnamurti who was speaking in Ojai, CA.

On a day in mid-May 1985, my wife and I went to hear Krishnamurti, who was speaking at a place called Oakgrove in Ojai. This was the first time I heard JK. He was over ninety; his hands trembled a little because of Parkinson's disease, but his mind was sharp. As usual he was chastising his audience about present centeredness and radical awareness, as he often did in his books.

One guy was heckling him, sort of. "Radical awareness does not come to us, Sir, so what should we do?"

Krishnamurti looked at him with his big kind eyes. He said gravely, with great dignity, "It must come."

Krishnamurti's "it" was the "presence" of which he spoke often -- enlightenment. The way he said the words though inspired me beyond belief.

That evening, my friend Frederica who was hosting my wife and I had honoured our desire to invite a friend of ours over. His name was Joel Morwood. We had met him the previous summer at Dr Wolf's ranch. Joel was a Hollywood producer and writer; but he'd heard the siren song, went on a quest, and was enlightened. He'd shared his experience with us, which was utterly believable. I respected and liked Joel.

That evening, Joel and I got into an argument, but fortunately it led to the most consequential experience of my life. I kept notes from which I am quoting:

> Joel and I got into a conversation about Reality. I was giving him an earful of my ideas about consciousness, arrived at from quantum theory, in terms of the theory of quantum measurement. Joel listened with attention. "So, what's next?" he asked.

"Well, I am not sure I understand how consciousness is manifest in the brain," I said, confessing my struggle with the idea that somehow consciousness must be an epiphenomenon of brain processes. "I think I understand consciousness, but..."

"Can consciousness be understood?" Joel interrupted me.

"It certainly can. I told you about how our conscious observation, consciousness, collapses the quantum wave..." I was ready to repeat the whole story.

But Joel stopped me. "So, is the brain of the observer prior to consciousness, or is consciousness prior to the brain?"

I saw a trap in his question. "I am talking about consciousness as the subject of our experiences."

"Consciousness is prior to experiences. It is without an object and without a subject."

Joel was making his trap wider. But I was the physicist; surely, I had answers better than his. He was just a filmmaker. So, I said not a little smugly, "Sure, that's vintage mysticism, but in my language, you are talking about some nonlocal aspect of consciousness."

Joel was not distracted by my terminology. Now he was visibly angry at my attempted sophistry. "You're wearing scientific blinders that keep you from understanding. Underneath, you have a belief that consciousness can be understood by science, that consciousness emerges in the brain, that it is an epiphenomenon. Comprehend what mystics are saying. Consciousness is prior and unconditioned. It is all there is. There is nothing but God." The last sentence he practically shouted at me.

That last sentence did something to me that is impossible to describe in words. The best that I can attempt is that it caused an abrupt change of perspective—as if a veil had lifted. Here was the answer I had been looking for and yet had known all along. *Consciousness is the ground of all being, and matter, including the brain, and consists of possibilities of consciousness itself to choose from.* And sure. One could do science with this basic metaphysics. I was sure of it.

This insight—consciousness is the ground of all being and matter consists of possibilities of consciousness itself to choose from—was all I needed to work out the basic theory of subject-object experience. Afterwards, I began writing a book on my insight, but for many years through many revisions I struggled in vain to find a publisher. Eventually, I wrote a scientific paper that was published in a physics Journal. In 1993, a book was finally published too, called *The Self-Aware Universe*.

V
The Camouflage the Physical Layer Creates

If consciousness is the ground of all being, then why don't we see it that way, why all the debate? When we understand how and why the camouflage, the puzzle gives way to a sense of wonder; *What shall I find if I penetrate this camouflage?*

You must go back to the time when mankind discovered science, the idea of verifying theory with experimental data and vice versa, not be fooled by what seems to be data until and unless we discover an explanation that can be verified. The experiments we could do then and the theories we discovered to explain them all, involved the macroworld. There was no entry in those days to the microworld.

Science began with the discovery of Newton's laws that govern the macroworld, the motion of bulk matter. The laws revealed that bulk matter has a state of natural motion— inertia. We also discovered that the agency of change is force; the changes the force produces are deterministic.

This fit the image of a clockwork universe. It gives us good reference points to live by. Our houses and furniture remain in the same place unless we move them.

Compare this with the possibility wave nature of the microworld. Possibility means uncertainty, indeterminacy. How can we be certain of where an object will be when it instantly becomes a wave of possibility whenever we are not looking at it?

And then confront one more puzzle. Matter is reductionistic: micro makes up macro, macro can be reduced to the micro. If micro is quantum, wave-like, could macro, which is made of micro, be any different? Where did all that freedom go?

The quantum equation of movement itself gave away the secret. When the mass of the quantum object becomes large, the waves do not expand very fast. In fact, macro-matter—

tables and houses (even if they were not cemented to the foundation) expand as waves so slowly that you have to wait for ten billion years to see a discernible movement. And that is just the motion of the centre of mass.

Here is a piece of useful information. The movement of composite objects can be broken down as a movement of the centre of mass in space and time, and then the relative movement of the internal objects about the centre of mass. Does that make sense? Make sure it does.

And here is the thing. The relative movement remains wave-like, but the different parts do not do their waving in synchrony anymore. They decohere. This phenomenon is called decoherence. Although the relative motion in a macro body remains as possibility, we can never verify that with an interference experiment like the double slit experiment.

In this way, the camouflage... If two people look at the same macro object within split seconds of each other as we do in public situations, we always find the object more or less at the same place. Then we compare and share the info and conclude that macro objects are objects of a shared external reality. If both of us see the same object in the same place, the object must be outside of both of us, right?

Of course, quantum physics still insists that these objects are wave-like. But what of it? If the wave aspect of the centre of mass is so subdued and the wave aspect of relative motion is not even measurable, why bother? This is the position scientific materialists take. They assert: macro objects *are* Newtonian. We don't need consciousness to choose the state they will manifest.

This is why theory is important. The assertion above is not theoretically correct. So, we should keep an open mind. When we do, we discover something unexpected. There is a difference between non-living and living macro matter. Whereas non-living bulk matter is approximately Newtonian, living matter is explicitly quantum because of their coupling with quantum objects. These quantum objects are objects of our internal experience— feelings and thoughts.

How do you penetrate the camouflage of physical matter being the one and only independent of consciousness? By looking at and exploring the internal objects of our experience. Millennia ago, the sage Patanjali introduced a practice called *pratyahara* in Sanskrit explained thus: as a tortoise withdraws his limbs within, similarly you withdraw your senses from looking at the external world and concentrate on the internal.

fig. 9: Two ways of knowing. Left: with open eyes, we get lost in the material world. Right: with closed eyes we become open to higher consciousness. Adapted from a cartoon in a book called *Precision Nirvana*

I show you my favourite cartoon the idea of which I found in a book called *Precision Nirvana* published in the nineteen eighties (fig. 9). Heed the message. Looking with open eyes will never enable you to penetrate the camouflage that the poet William Blake called "Newton's sleep." How do mystics penetrate it? They follow Patanjali's advice and close their eyes—Patanjali's sleep (also called meditation).

Chapter 3
Inward Journey: The Quantum Science of Experience

I
Tangled Hierarchy

In 1980, the artificial Intelligence researcher Doug Hofstadter wrote a book named *Gödel, Escher, Bach: The Eternal Golden Braid* in which he proposed a recipe for building a conscious computer. He called the recipe tangled hierarchy.

The concept of simple hierarchy (fig. 2 is an example) I have already introduced. The reductionist nature of matter is a simple hierarchy because cause flows only one way—bottom up. Two levels form a tangled hierarchy when they are connected by a circular cause; in other word they cause each other.

An example makes it clear. Consider the sentence *I am a liar*. *I* and *liar* are called subject and predicate respectively in grammar; the predicate refers to the subject according to the rules of grammar. However, here when the predicate refers to the subject, there is a contradiction, If I am a liar, then I am telling the truth. Go back to the subject again, contradiction also: if I am telling the truth, I am lying. The sentence forces you to reverberate back and forth between the predicate and subject; you are caught in the sentence. The sentence now has a self: you have lent your own self to the sentence.

But of course, the trap has created only an illusion of your identity with the sentence; you have created the trap for yourself by following the rules of English grammar. But you don't have to. You can jump out of identifying with the sentence any time you like.

Hofstadter says the sentence is a tangled hierarchy and you are the inviolate level. In truth you at the inviolate level have created the tangled hierarchy via the imposition of the rules of English grammar with the two poles—subject and predicate—seeming to continuously recreate the other.

Hofstadter's idea had little impact on the AI researchers; a tangled hierarchy is impossible to create in human made hardware. I read Hofstadter's book in 1981 and immediately saw that if applied to our brain, it solves the problem of how I can inject my own self into my brain.

Suppose the brain has two apparatuses in it that form a tangled hierarchy. When I try to look at objects through the brain's eyes, I get trapped in its tangled hierarchy, does that not make sense?

It does and it doesn't. It does because I now identify with the brain and consider myself as a separate being—subject—separate from the rest of the world of objects. My consciousness has split into two—subject and object—giving me an experience. I have a theory of how experiences come about.

It doesn't because our individual ego does not seem to act tangled hierarchically, does it? If you inspect, you will readily discover that what you call ego has various personality programmes and you are the head honcho running the programmes as you wish. This is a description of simple hierarchy.

It doesn't also because it sounds like dualism. Dualism aside, there is also that paradox I referred to before with this von Neumann-Wolf-and now Goswami way of thinking. Physicist Eugene Wigner pointed out the paradox; it is called paradox of Wigner's friend.

Suppose there is a two-valued quantum traffic light with two possibilities: red and green (never mind that such a quantum traffic light may be impossible to build) and you are approaching it from one road. Simultaneously so is your friend but from the perpendicular road (fig. 10). And of course, being busy people of modern culture who bore easily, you both want green, choose green. If you both get to choose, collision! But if only one of you gets to choose, whose choice is it that counts?

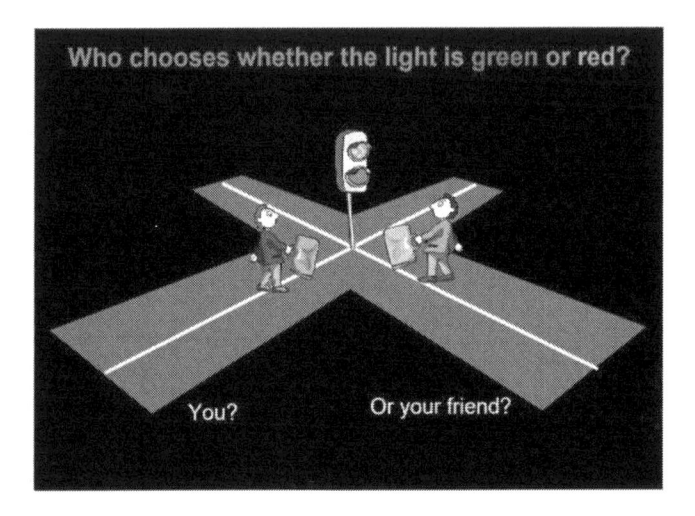

fig. 10: The paradox of Wigner's friend: who gets to choose green?

The fact is there is no way to settle this dispute. No criterion can be given unless you are the only conscious being and everybody else is your extension as in the following story popularized by comedian Bette Meddler.

A Hollywood woman is walking the famous Sunset Boulevard in Hollywood when she comes across a friend that she has not met in years. "Oh, let's catch up with each other over a cup of coffee." They find a coffee house, are served, and she starts talking. After half hour, her awareness returns and she says, "Oh look at me, all this time talking about myself. Let's talk about you. What do you think of me?"

Philosophy has a name for this supposed phenomenon: solipsism. Yes, people do behave like they are solipsists, they are the only consciousness around, everyone else is their extension. But of course, that does not make solipsism right.

In effect, this paradox of who gets to choose seems to kill the von Neumann theory of how collapse works through our observer consciousness and so also my little theory of experience.

Everything changed when I discovered the real origin of quantum collapse: it is not our individual consciousness, but consciousness that is the ground of all being that chooses. That chooses from its own possibilities, no dualism. *Collapse is nonlocal, no signals need to be exchanged.*

When this nonlocal consciousness sees through the tangled hierarchical brain and identifies with the brain being caught in the tangled hierarchy, it produces a representation of unity consciousness, a unity self that I call quantum self. The simple hierarchy of the ego is created via conditioning and our habit of being conscious of being conscious before. Read my book with Valentina Onisor, *The Quantum Brain*.

Nonlocal collapse creates the subject-object split of one consciousness (fig. 11). The subject and the object arise together—dependent co-arising—a concept found in the Buddhist literature written millennia ago. How amazing is that?

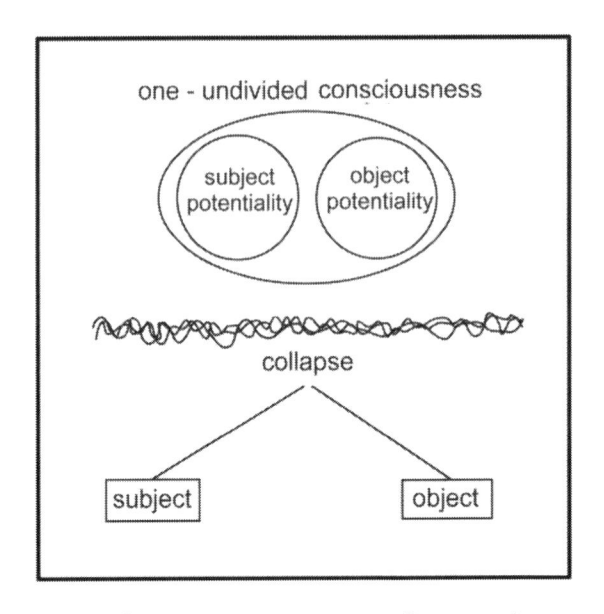

[Diagram: "one - undivided consciousness" containing "subject potentiality" and "object potentiality", with a wavy line labeled "collapse" splitting into "subject" and "object"]

fig. 11: With quantum measurement, One consciousness gives rise to the duality of a subject-object split

Is the subject an appearance? Of course it is, those *mayabadis* (people who declare that the world we experience is illusory seen through an illusory subject) are not all wrong. It took me a few more years to identify them, but the two brain apparatuses that make up its tangled hierarchy are the brain's perception and the memory apparatuses. Notice the tangle: perception creates memory (obvious) and memory creates perception (requires some explanation).

Memory creates one-way-ness of time. The equations of physics work equally well in both directions of time. In this way, the potentialities have no one-way time marker; they can grow and undo the growth equally well. But once collapsed and a memory is created, the experience cannot be undone, it is irreversible. In this way, without memory there is no perception (every attempt to do so will undo itself).

Now you can appreciate a depiction of tangled hierarchy created by the artist M.C. Escher, *Drawing Hands* (fig. 12). Left hand seems to draw the right, and vice versa. And it is an appearance; behind the scene, Escher is drawing both from the inviolate level.

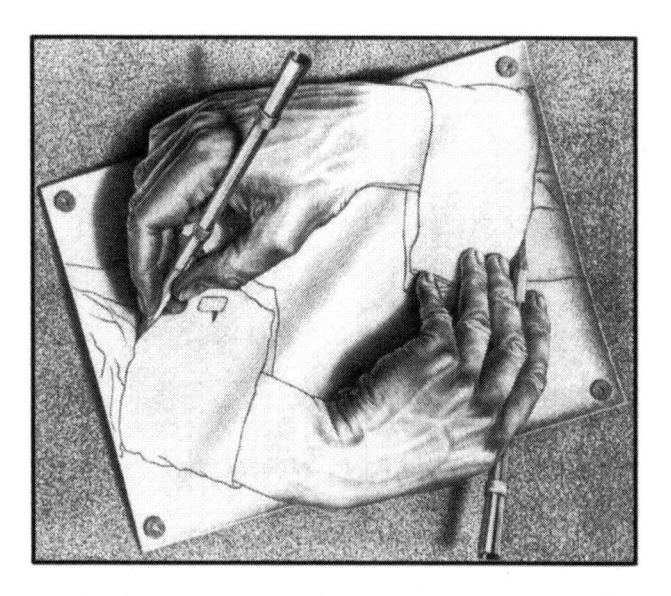

fig. 12: *Drawing Hands* by M. C. Escher. Artist's rendition.

The tangle arises because from the manifest level, consciousness assumes it has to collapse one apparatus at a time, thus creating the trap and identifying with it, getting caught in it. Actually, from behind the scene, the unity consciousness collapses both apparatuses at once.

Notice what happens when consciousness disengages with the trap; it is back to the unity consciousness once again. There is no longer any experience, the unmanifest is unconscious. The unmanifest domain of potentiality that consciousness presides over is our unconscious. As you know, the concept of the unconscious in modern psychology was discovered by Freud for whom the unconscious consists of individual suppressed and repressed memory. Then Carl

Jung generalized the concept to include an additional collective unconscious—mankind's collective memory. And quantum science is expanding the concept further to include all those previously uncollapsed potentialities as well, making room for creativity.

One further note in passing. All this is included in a somewhat primitive form in my book *The Self-Aware Universe*. A few researchers, transpersonal psychologists mainly, noticed it. I got a call of affirmation from Stan Grof almost immediately after publication. But the hard scientists of the brain never acknowledged my work; they still don't.

Fortunately, the philosopher David Chalmers did us all a favour. At a consciousness conference in 1994, he challenged the neuroscientists with what is now called *the hard question*: how can a science of objects answer the question, how does experience arise since experience also has a subject pole and a subject cannot possibly be explained when you only have objects to work with?

II
The Quantum Self and the Ego

There is also the ego—our everyday experience of the self, individual and personal. The quantum self, the representation of unity consciousness in the brain, loses its universality via reflection in the mirror of memory before we experience it. The reflection occurs in two stages: 1) In the first stage, via a process of stimulus-response-reinforcement, learning takes place giving us habit patters and character traits; the processing here takes about half a second.

2) In the second stage, we apply our character in different situations, reconstruct our memories a bit here and there, and develop various personality programmes for ourselves to respond suitably to the situation. In this way we become the head honcho, the boss of our programmes, a simple hierarchy. This is the everyday self—call it ego/character/persona—that we experience.

Fig. 13 shows you the difference between the quantum self and the ego. The following image from the Upanishad helps to see the difference:

> Two birds, united always, and known by the same name, closely cling to the same tree. One of them eats the sweet fruit; the other looks on without eating.

Ok, we have given the two birds—aspects--of the same self--different names; that is easy. The real difference between the ego and the quantum self, says this verse, is that whereas the ego programmes are needed to eat the fruit of *samsara*, the manifest world, the quantum self is the connection to Oneness indifferent to the manifest world.

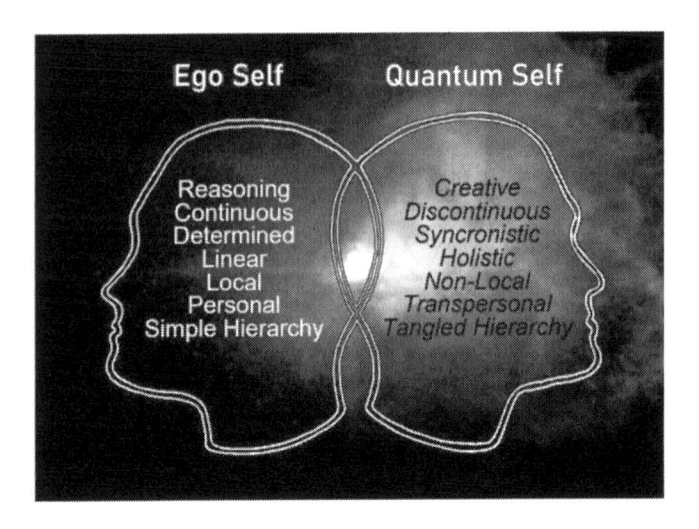

Ego Self — Reasoning, Continuous, Determined, Linear, Local, Personal, Simple Hierarchy

Quantum Self — Creative, Discontinuous, Syncronistic, Holistic, Non-Local, Transpersonal, Tangled Hierarchy

fig. 13: The Quantum Self and Ego

Let me end this section with a Zen story that covers both aspects of the self; the story gives an example each of quantum self-action and the ego-action, examples to remember. Two monks were about to cross a muddy river. A high current was making it muddy, but the river was not really very deep, quite walkable. Just then, a maiden appeared on the scene in a beautiful attire that went all the way to her ankles. Naturally, the maiden was hesitating to step into the river lest her clothes get ruined. One of the monks asked for her permission and when she nodded, picked her right up and walked across the river and put her down. The maiden thanked the monk and went her way. The other monk soon caught up with the first and they both continued on their way.

After about an hour the second monk spoke. "Brother, you did something very wrong back there, you know. We monks are not supposed to touch women, let alone carry them for so long as it took you to go across the river, a full five minutes, and you held her so close."

The first monk said, "Brother, I carried the maiden for five minutes, but you are still carrying her."

The first monk performed an act of compassion responding to his intuition that the maiden was desperately in need of help. When we respond to our intuition, we act from the quantum self. The second monk was thinking from his conditioned ego and the programme of his judging mind. So, he suffered.

III
Subtle Experiences

At the risk of beating my own drum, the discovery within quantum physics that consciousness is the ground of all being was a major breakthrough, a scientific milestone, a beginning of a new consciousness-based paradigm. This new science, which for a while I called *Science within consciousness* but have now renamed the simpler *Quantum Science*, integrates science and the wisdom traditions that began 7000 years ago in India with the revelation of the Upanishads, also called the Vedanta. However, there was much struggle ahead before there was a complete rapprochement between Vedanta and my work.

After my discovery, I was busy first, to develop a paradox-free interpretation of quantum physics featuring primacy of consciousness and second, writing a book on the subject (it took me some seven drafts) and a scientific paper. I also felt compelled to write a textbook on quantum physics and present my ideas to contemporary and future professionals as much as the referees would allow.

Only after this flurry of activities was finished did I turn to catching up with the Vedanta literature. An invitation to speak at the Vivekananda Kendra in Bangalore, India provided additional incentive and that revealed the idea of *panchakosha*—five sheaths. I only had two of the sheaths so far: the bottom one and the top one. What about the other three?

Majority of scientists still believe that mind is brain and this was early 1990s, then this belief was widespread. There were a few exceptions; the Nobelist Roger Sperry was one who brought up the idea of a meaning processing mind in the early 1980s. But it was the reading of John Searle's work, *The Rediscovery of the Mind*, that convinced me that brain looked upon as a computer can represent meaning as symbols but does not or cannot process, that is, understand, meaning. Our mind is needed for that. Mind is non-physical. In the nineties, Roger Penrose supported Searle's idea with powerful math of Gödel's theorem: any elaborate mathematical system is either inconsistent or incomplete.

Accordingly, I wrote two papers positing that meaning-processing mind was quantum in nature and demonstrating the veracity of the idea with some cognitive data. The papers were published in *The Journal of Mind and Behavior.* A UCLA professor wrote a critique of my ideas and the journal published both the critique and my rebuttal of it.

I was also making some progress in the vital energy front. Here the problem was two-fold: 1) Experiencing vital energy; people told me excitedly about their experiences of it, but nobody was giving me any hints about how to experience it. And 2) Nobody knew any scientific concept explaining vital energy in clear scientific terms.

The problem of experiencing vital energy was solved in two steps. In 1981, I got a call from my fellow consciousness researchers in the psych department of the U of O. They needed me since I was a hard scientist, for testing out the veracity of a fellow who was claiming that he can demonstrate vital energy. Of course, I went. The fellow looked like a hippie but friendly; his girlfriend was with him. Indeed, he claimed that his palms were "energized," and he challenged each one of us to put our palms in between his energized palms. "You will feel tingles," he said, "That is vital energy."

Oh, yeah? One by one my psych friends went and put their palms between the palms of the fellow. But they shook their heads. Nothing, no tingles. I was the last. Imagine my surprise when I felt quite pronounced tingles; I even verified it by withdrawing my palms, waiting for a pause, and trying again. The tingles were unmistakable.

When I shared my experience with my colleagues, they wouldn't believe me. Instead I lost my credibility with some of them who started referring to me as a mystical physicist.

Ok, so I experienced vital energy but I still could not produce it at will. All that changed when I attended a workshop with the famous physician/mystic Richard Moss in Lone Pine, CA, the same place where I met Franklin Wolff. The same year, 1983.

Richard himself with his colleagues gave each one of us a "chakra healing" with energized palms, much like the other fellow. Well, afterwards, there was a session, and people, there were twenty-six of us, were telling their experiences in glorious terms. I, who had hardly any experience, felt totally left out. Like "What am I doing here?" Finally, I could not hold it any longer and raised my arm.

"Yes, Amit."

"Richard, looks like you gave all these experiences to all these people, why not me?"

Richard said, "Amit, I can only open the door for you. It is you who has to pass through it."

"Sounds well and dandy. So, you are saying all these people passed through the door and I chose not to."

"That's for you to decide. All these people left their selves at the door. That's the trick. Then you enter."

"But I am a scientist. I want to be there when it happens." I blurted out. Everybody was laughing LOL in today's language. And I realized my mistake. In the next few days I received ample doses of Richard's prescription medicine—juicy physicality consisting of intimate hugs, especially from women. After that and a few more sessions of chakra healing, I got it. I could feel tingles when I rubbed my palms together. I could experience energy even in my chakras.

Now my curiosity was really aroused. What is the science behind those feelings of vital energy? Energy usually means something is moving. What exactly? Then, I read Rupert Sheldrake's book, *A New Science of Life* and a veil lifted. In this book, Sheldrake theorizes that nonphysical fields that he called morphogenetic fields are crucial to explain how biological organs get their form and functions. Aha! I thought. Vital energy must be the movement of these morphogenetic fields.

Immediately I saw biological organs differently from non-living matter. I saw them as exhibiting both law-like and program-like behaviour whereas non-living matter is strictly law-like. The law-like behaviour corresponds to the chemical hardware of the organ; the software is the contribution of the morphogenetic fields except that they have more to do with organ functions and less to do with form where some "laws of form" may also play a role. The Greek root word for function is liturgy; so I call these fields as liturgical or more elaborately liturgical/morphogenetic fields. Think of them as vital software; every physical organ P-organ has a vital counterpart V-organ non-locally correlated with it (Fig. 14). When consciousness collapses a physical organ function, it also collapses the correlated vital organ. It is this movement of the liturgical/morphogenetic fields that we feel as vital energy. See chapter 7 for further details.

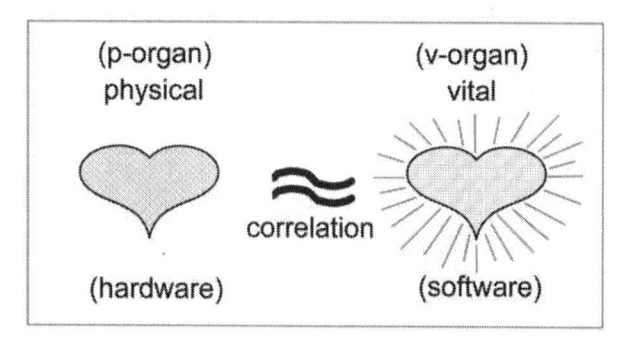

fig. 14: Every physical p-organ has a correlated v-organ

IV
Descartes' Errors and the Importance of Intuition

In Indian wisdom tradition, consciousness has more or less always been recognized as a major player of reality. In the dualist philosophy of Samkhya on which the Yoga tradition is based, the duo *purush*a and *prakriti* are said to be the precursors of our subject-object experience of duality. However, you can easily see these concepts as intermediaries that nondual consciousness uses in order to manifest the subject-object experience. Indeed, Samkhya is sometimes called qualified nondualism. In quantum science, purusha can be seen as subject-potentiality of the observer's brain and prakriti as object-potentiality in the nondual consciousness that Vedanta calls Brahman. All that is different from pure Vedanta is that Brahman is now qualified by the laws of manifestation.

It has been a different journey for the Westerners; here Descartes dictum "I think therefore, I am," made consciousness a part of the mental experience. Cartesian dualism is a dualism of mind and body—both sound like objects of experience. The subject-pole is shoved into the background.

The influence of Descartes' Interaction Dualism of Mind and Body was far and wide albeit its fundamental ontological problem: the interaction between a non-material mind and a material body requires a mediator, but where is it?

There are other problems too with Descartes' philosophy. For Descartes, mind is about thinking. More recently, Western researchers have complained about Descartes' error and have insisted that we correct the error by expanding the concept of mind to the concept of a psyche of all inner experiences—both thinking and feeling.

In the eighteenth century, the philosophy of idealism with consciousness in the foreground re-entered Western thinking in the form of a philosophy propounded by the famous Bishop George Berkeley: ideas come first. All our knowledge about the physical world undeniably comes via the intermediary of mental ideas.

Eventually, the problem with Berkeley's teachings was summarized beautifully in a one-liner question: If a tree falls in the forest but no one is around to hear it, is there a sound of the tree falling?

The question is diabolically clever. According to physical laws, there has to be a sound. But how can Berkeley account for the sound without having anybody to hear the sound? Berkeley came up with the quip: there is always God's mind.

God's mind, our mind, it is all mixed up in the traditional "Western" mind. Forget traditions and see that there is no Western versus Eastern mind in the laws of consciousness. Recognize that God's mind is consciousness.

Recognize also that the human mind has "many mansions," not just one, thinking. Not even two, thinking and feeling. But three. The third internal experience is intuition and the objects that we intuit, were called archetypes by Plato, and virtue by wisdom traditions; the Upanishads call them experiences of Vi-*gyana*—contexts of *gyana* (knowledge). Aurobindo called them supramental. In quantum science we sometimes call them supramental-supravital and sometimes as archetypal. Rose by any name...

But materialists have another model for the nature of intuition. Best to illustrate this model with a story. You have seen those big, tall cylinders of the boiler room of any industrial establishment. In one such establishment, the boiler was not working properly, so they called an engineer to fix it. The engineer looked at the problem, and then tapped the cylinder, and all was fixed. Later he sent his bill of $1007. The recipients were indignant with the amount of the bill: "All you did was to tap."

The engineer wrote back: You are right and I did accordingly, charge only $7 for the tapping. The $1000 is for intuiting *where* to tap.

According to materialists, intuition is just part of the experts' strategy: all experts memorize thousands upon thousands of case histories of each and every problem and their solution that worked. That's where their intuition comes from.

I learned about intuition first hand at the age of three. My mother had an interesting way of teaching numbers. First, she taught me to count up to a hundred. Next, she tried to teach me connection of numbers and how they pertain to counting physical objects. 2 cows, but the same number 2 could be talking about two pencils. She was trying to teach me the concept behind numbers what mathematicians call set theory. I would not be able to explain it at the age of 3, but I intuited the concept all right. Later when I formally learned set theory, I found that what I intuited was right on the dot.

The same thing you can try with the concept of infinity. Hungarians joke about yokels who cannot learn numbers beyond 3. For them it is 1, 2, 3, infinity. But you know what? 3 is as far away from infinity as 10^{100}. You don't get to infinity by conceiving large numbers; you do it by intuition.

Intuitions are an essential component of understanding mathematics. Mathematical intuitions beat rational thinking about numbers: this is the purport of the famous Gödel's theorem.

The objects of intuition are called archetypes—Plato's term for the contexts of highest rational knowledge—*vigyana*. What do we know about them?

I became aware of the Platonic term upon reading a chapter in Richard Feynman's marvellous book, *The Character of Physical Law*. Yes, the same Richard Feynman who proposed that scientists accept wearing the straightjacket of scientific materialism to take science forward. But you see, Feynman himself probably never did wear such a straightjacket because in this book he suggests that Plato's idea of archetype is the best explanation of where physical laws come from—from the land of archetypes, specifically the archetype of Truth. More on archetypes later (see chapter 8).

V
The Tibetan Book of the Dead is Correct; it is your job to prove it

The title of this section came to me as part of a dream; believe it, it was important. It was while trying to prove that *The Tibetan Book of the Dead* is correct that I finally conceptually penetrated the physical sheath of reality.

Understanding experiences of thoughts and feelings as movements of a nonphysical mind and a nonphysical vital body was intellectually satisfying, but it opened the door for dualism once again. Let's face it. Sheldrake morphogenetic fields guide the development of form and function of the physical organ, says Sheldrake giving an analogy of electromagnetic waves affecting a radio set. Except that there are no known local signals that mediate between the morphogenetic fields he posits and the physical organ! In the absence of any mediator, it is just dualism. In the same way, nonphysical mental memories of thoughts constitute mental software of brain's neuronal circuits of hardware. But in the absence of a specified mediator, this is also dualism.

And then a series of synchronicities took place that attracted my attention to an unexpected but important problem—reincarnation--for the integration of science and spirituality. It is while trying to solve this problem that enabled me to solve the problem of dualism.

The synchronicities began in 1993 after my first book on the new paradigm *The Self-Aware Universe* came out; I was on my very first radio show when this old lady asked me, "What happens when we die?" I didn't know! The question took me aback, it is embarrassing for an academic to profess ignorance but I recovered and soon forgot about the question. I was not ready.

A month or so later, an elderly Theosophist started taking a reading course from me on *The Self-Aware Universe*. But in truth, he only started to fill *my* head with ideas such as reincarnation important in Theosophical thought. At first, I did not take the subject seriously. Then as I was dreaming one night, I heard something. It was as if a voice was speaking to me. The voice grew louder and louder. Soon it became an admonition I could clearly hear, "*The Tibetan Book of the Dead* is correct; it's your job to prove it." The admonition was so loud it woke me up. *The Tibetan Book of the Dead* is a guide to the "experiences" of the surviving "soul" between death and rebirth. I started taking survival after death and reincarnation seriously after this dream.

Another couple of months later, a graduate student, whose boyfriend had died came to my office for help with her grieving. I told her that I was no therapist or healer but she insisted on talking with me and kept coming back. Then one day, I was trying to say to her by way of consolation that maybe her boyfriend's subtle body—mind, vital, and all that essence, all nonphysical to be sure—survived his death, an idea I had picked up from my Hindu upbringing but never took seriously because of inherent dualism: how do physical and nonphysical interact without a mediator? Suddenly a thought came to me—suppose both the physical and the subtle essence of a person consists of quantum possibilities and consciousness mediates between them non-locally, without exchanging signals? Could that not solve the problem of dualism as well as that of survival? Subsequently, I wrote a book *Physics of the soul*—a book with a scientific theory of reincarnation and an explanation of the *Tibetan book of the Dead.*

VI
The Quantum Psychophysical Parallelism

Back to my discovery of quantum science's answer to dualism. Consciousness is the ground of all being: the sensing experience of the physical, the experience of feelings of the vital universe, the experience of meaning of the mental sheath, the experience of intuition from the archetypal layer of the world. The objects of experience—sensory objects of matter, the liturgical/morphogenetic fields of the vital, the meanings of the mind, the archetypes of the supramental-supravital—all exist as potentialities of consciousness to choose from. When consciousness chooses, we have experiences of sensing, feeling, thinking, and intuiting.

Jung did a study of personality types from his vast repertoire of clients and came up with a four-type classification of personalities (fig. 15). This supports that there are indeed four kinds of experiences.

```
              INTUITION
    FEELING  ⬄  THINKING
              SENSATION
```

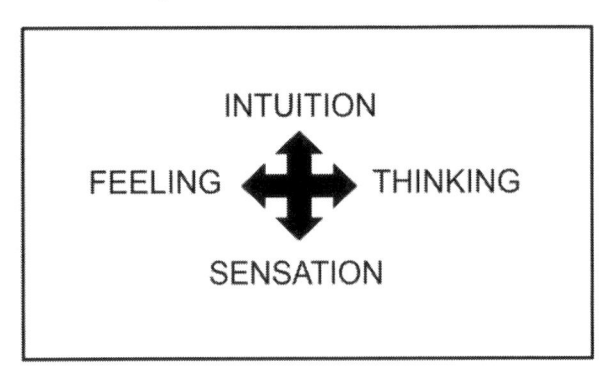

fig. 15: Jung's typology of human personalities

Be clear about one thing. The material potentialities we sense are approximately Newtonian; they are virtually "determined" potentiality causing confusion. Just because, whenever we look at the moon, it appears more or less exactly where we expect it, does not mean it is out there independent of our looking!

Nothing is ever out there. Only actuality is that which happens, and all happens in here, inside our consciousness. The material experience appears to be outside. Why? Because a material macro body's potentiality is approximately determined; you and I both virtually see it at the same place so we can reach a consensus about it. Material sensory objects are experienced as public creating the illusion that they are outside of us.

In contrast, the vital, mental, supramental potentialities are experienced as internal and private. Between my experience of a thought or a feeling or an intuition, the potentialities change so much that you or I could not possibly choose the same thought, or feeling, or intuition.

What does that mean? Simply that the vital, mental and supramental-supravital potentialities are truly quantum.

These ideas I call quantum psycho-physical parallelism. Think of consciousness in its ground of being, the unconscious as consisting of four separate worlds of potentiality all going on in parallel. When consciousness responds to a stimulus, it may have a response in more than the world where the stimulus originates. In this way, our experiences—responses to stimuli— are often a mixture of two or more of the four varieties.

Specifically, we never experience the physical without simultaneously experiencing the feeling of the sensation or the meaning of it. In other word, perception is impossible with some way to cognize: this is what we do with feeling and/or meaning.

Intuitions also come to us only in association with a feeling or meaning or both. Intuitions come to some people with a shiver in the spine, either as a gut feeling and a thought or as a feeling in the heart along with a thought. But of course, if we are not sensitive to feeling, we may notice just the thought—intuitive thought. But even so we can clearly tell that this thought is different from an ordinary rational thought.

Jesus said, ask and you shall find; and when you find you will be troubled. Exactly my point. Although your feelings remain obscure, they trouble you! "Here is some important message I must investigate further." In this way, intuitions are doorways to creative explorations of new meaning and noble feelings.

Why do intuitions need to come to us riding on thinking and/or feeling? This is because we have no direct way of representing intuitions as memories in any place in the body, not even the brain.

There was a great philosopher named Gottfried Leibniz, a contemporary of Newton, who actually figured out some of this parallel processing of our various experiences. He proposed psychophysical parallelism as a solution for the critique of Cartesian interactionism—the problem of the mediator. He proposed the psyche and the physical go on in parallel and was immediately criticized: what maintains the parallelism in view of all the dynamism of the human experiences such as creativity?

The idea of interacting quantum psychophysical parallelism, as I introduce here, solves the problem. Consciousness maintains the parallelism as it also mediates the interaction between the parallel worlds as they manifest. And all this through nonlocality without any exchange of signals.

The good news is that Jung's discovery, the phenomenon of synchronicities--meaningful coincidences consisting of one external and one internal event, both caused by their common cause of manifestation, consciousness--widely experienced by people (read my own story again reported in the previous sections if you need more convincing) supports the idea proposed here (fig. 16).

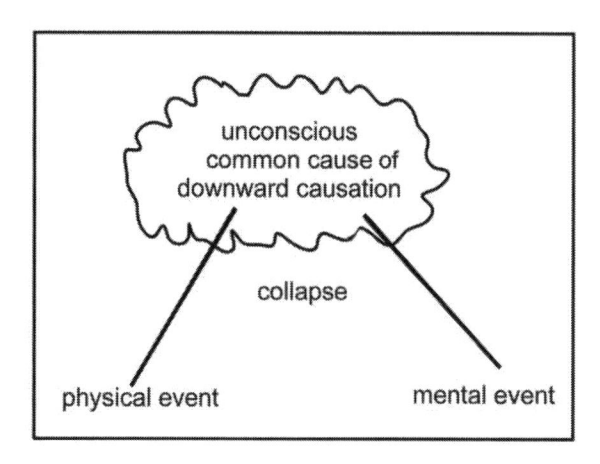

fig. 16: Synchronicity is always a coincidence between a physical event and a meaningful mental event

Synchronistic events happen to everyone in need of a breakthrough, in connection with romance, therapy, creativity, meaning-of-life questions in general, just to name a few contexts.

If you want to incorporate meaning and purpose in your life, synchronicity offers you a viable means. As the neuroscientist John Lilly used so say, "Expect the unexpected," and synchronicities will come.

VII
Does Quantum Physics Apply to us?

Many biologists think that the "subatomic events are too small to have a practical importance." Other scientists object in the same vein: "electrons and people are not the same thing".

There is no doubt that ultimately, quantum physics rules all matter, micro and macro. However, for practical purposes, we must recognize that for bulk matter Newton's physics approximately rules. This, too, is part of the quantum dynamics applied to matter; it is called the correspondence principle.

What this means is that at the bulk macro level, matter is still wave like, but the wave nature is much subdued leaving consciousness with very little possibility to choose from. Face it; bulk inanimate matter is largely independent of consciousness.

Living matter is different though, it has vitality. A living body is a dynamic duo of a physical component and a vital component. *It is the vital component that is quantum; the physical is quantum by association.*

To understand things better, a little more quantum physics is needed. The turning point for our understanding of quantum physics came with the 1982 experimental verification by Alain Aspect and his collaborators of a 1935 theoretical idea of three physicists: Albert Einstein, Boris Podolsky, and Nathan Rosen. This EPR message is crucial to understand, fortunately not the mathematics.

(I once met Boris Podolsky's son, a fellow named Pan Podolsky. He claimed that his father Boris, at the time a graduate student of Einstein, had the original idea which Einstein and his post-doc Nathan Rosen abducted, a frequent complaint of graduate students.)

The message of EPR is simple: if two quantum objects—waves of possibility—come close and interact they become correlated or entangled. What this means is that they develop an unusual purely quantum characteristic of instant communication which remains intact even when they are not interacting, even when they move far away, even galaxies apart, from each other. We call such instant communication nonlocal.

Uncorrelated objects in space and time, they are particles, they do not have this characteristic. Objects in space and time require signals to communicate; signals have a speed limit, the speed of light. Signals travel with a finite speed taking a finite time from one locality to another through the intervening space. Objects in space and time generally are objects with separateness.

In contrast, if the waves of potentiality are correlated, then, when they are actualized as particles, their behavior indicates that they have communicated instantly, without signals. How could they have done that? Because, you must realize, the correlation or entanglement made them into one. One does not need a signal to communicate with itself. Their oneness reflects the oneness of consciousness; consciousness maintains their oneness even at a distance.

The oneness of objects in the domain of potentiality is a potential oneness. EPR gave us the clue how to actualize and thereby verify the oneness via measurements in space and time.

The vital-physical duo, living bodies, are correlated quantum objects. They are one. When we experience a physical organ, we also experience the movement of its correlated vital organ (see fig. 14). The experience of this movement is called feeling. Vitality, call it the movement vital energy, is a feeling.

We are saying vital movements are quantum; therefore, the movements of physical macro living bodies, the organs, are also quantum by virtue of correlation. In this way, by virtue of its vital connection, every living organ (including the organs of the brain) offers quantum possibilities for consciousness to choose from, consciousness chooses, and an experience is born.

Amazingly, the *rishis* of India five thousand years ago intuited as much. They too predicted that we need three worlds: the causal world of consciousness, the gross world of matter to make representations, and the subtle world for connecting the two.

Chapter 4
The Second Layer of Manifest Reality: The Vital Body

I
Liturgical Fields

We experience the vital world through feelings. It gets confusing because there is clear difference between male and female in how they experience the world; and yet, who can deny that to interact with the opposite sex is one of the best ways to learn about the vital world. I illustrate this difference quoting a comic strip called *Pickles*. In the first two frames the wife says, "It is funny, on the inside I feel one way, but when I look into the mirror, I feel different from how I look on the outside." On the third frame she adds, "You know what I mean?" "Huh," exclaims the husband, "On the outside I looked like I was listening, but on the inside, I was thinking about corndogs."

In other words, women feel and think and men just think. I was one of these men myself, I know. I remember attending a talk by a new age self-avowed enlightened teacher. When a woman disciple asked his advice about how to handle emotions, he answered squarely, "Emotions don't exist."

I don't think most of us men would go that far. For most of us, negative emotions like anger are common experiences, but of course the common sense wisdom is that emotions are some kind of thought, certainly are brain phenomena. This much, men in all Western cultures know: Emotions are inefficient. Men are taught early to suppress negative emotions, nay, all emotions.

Are emotions solely brain phenomena? Women talk about pure feelings in the heart that they call love, feelings without thought, no kidding. Men usually dismiss women's experience.

But men's normal reaction aside, how do feelings arise in the body? My second wife challenged me to experience love in my heart; that set me off in a personal journey of discovery of feelings in the body, which I did, thanks to the spiritual teacher Richard Moss. That was 1983.

But I got side-tracked and abandoned the quest toward understanding feelings and emotions. Only in 1993, when the problem of dualism about including nonphysical experiences in science was solved, could I return once again to ask, *now that I have experienced feelings in the body at places that Easterners call chakras, is there any scientific explanation of these phenomena of feelings and chakras?*

I mentioned before how my reading of Rupert Sheldrake's book *A New Science of Life* helped me understand feelings of vital energy. Of course, Sheldrake, like most biologists, would never engage in the concept of vital energy. Vital energy is a forbidden concept in modern biology. Sheldrake had other motivations: he was aware of humankind's collective memory represented in Carl Jung's concept of the collective unconscious. He was also aware of Lamarck's theory of evolution of acquired characteristic as in ostrich's knee and human beings' hardened sole of the feet. Most of all he was keenly aware of the phenomenon of cell differentiation. He wanted to find biological explanations of these phenomena.

Let's talk about the phenomenon of cell differentiation. We are all born as a one-celled embryo called the zygote. All cells of the body result from the cell division of this one cell with identical DNA and identical genetic codes to make proteins. And yet cells in different parts of the body belonging to different organs make only proteins relevant for that organ function. The toe will make proteins suitable for walking; the liver cells make proteins to help digestion; the brain cells make proteins to help us perceive and make memory. How does the cell know where it is in the body, to which organ it belongs?

Sheldrake's creativity gave him the insight that a new nonphysical organizing principle in the form of morphogenetic fields must come into play to produce cell differentiation—cells in different organs making different proteins. *Morph* means form in Greek; genesis of course means creation. In this way Sheldrake conceptualized this organizing principle as a force field responsible for the epigenetic guidance of genes that regulated which functional genes are going to be turned "on" to make the proteins appropriate for a given organ form and function. In other words, there is a physical hardware of the organ, but a nonphysical software, V-organ guides them.

It is now generally agreed that there are indeed epigenetic mechanisms that affect organ development and function. Sheldrake is saying that there is no physical mechanism for doing this; hence the idea of a nonphysical morphogenetic field is needed. Materialists say, the biochemical environment of the organ itself provides the guidance. Undoubtedly, there must be a role for the environment, that cannot be denied.

Nevertheless, I agree with Sheldrake. Biological forms and functions are purposive, not causal. The software being purposive could not be easily made by physical causal forces. All proposed evolutionary and developmental scenarios based on scientific materialism tax our imagination. On the other hand, consciousness can choose actuality from possibility toward a purpose.

So here is my revision of Sheldrake's basic idea: these fields are not just morphogenetic; they are also liturgical—functional (remember? liturgy in Greek means function), consciousness uses them as epigenetic blueprints to guide the physical hardware toward desired form and function in spite of environmental interactions and interventions.

The name "liturgical" was the contribution of chi gong master Konstantin Pavlides. One day after a joint workshop, while I was complaining to him about the misnomer

Sheldrake uses for denoting these fields of purposive structures and functions, he suggested, "Why not change the name?" He looked up the Greek word liturgical for function from an etymology dictionary.

All this was revision of an original idea due to Sheldrake. My original idea, an authentic theory of feeling, was this: wherever there is a biological organ, consciousness has programmed the organ with software consisting of specific liturgical field/blueprint. This liturgical field/blueprint of biological software becomes forever correlated (that is, they communicate non-locally) with the physical. In this way, for every P-organ (P for physical), there is a correlated V-organ – V for vital (see fig. 14).

I will never forget the night when a conceptual understanding of the chakras dawned in me. I had a friend who lived in a Maryland suburb of Washington D.C. I was visiting Washington; this friend had invited me along with a bunch of health professionals from nearby NIH, National Institute of Health. My friend's wife who was a researcher at NIH wanted to hear along with her friends my ideas about quantum physics and consciousness.

When the time of presentation came, I asked the gathering somewhat sheepishly, "Would anybody mind if I changed the subject to a theory of chakras, a new scientific theory that I just discovered?"

There was initially some scepticism. Somebody asked, "Chakras are where we feel feelings; what does quantum physics have to do with feelings?"

I told him about Sheldrake's morphogenetic fields. "Nonphysical morphogenetic fields help consciousness to make programmes for organ functioning. It is the quantum movement of these fields, call it vital energy, that we feel. Vital energy is pure quantum energy."

"I still don't get it," the questioner continued. "I feel love; what does that got to do with organ function?"

"Everything," said I. "When two people fall in love, their immune systems make a contract to suspend their function."

That got everybody's attention. After I finished my talk, there was agreement, and then even some applause. Of course, being expatriated Indians, they all knew quite a bit about the chakras. The surprise was that I was proclaiming a scientific theory for the chakras and was able to answer their many sceptical inquiries satisfactorily. There was even some genuine respect. Below I give the theory, modified of course by many years of continuing insights. But first some comments about the vital body.

What constitutes our Vital Body and what makes it a Sheath?

All the vital software associated with the physical organs of our body makes us what we call our vital body. We feel the movement of the vital software when actualized as vitality, vital energy. Part of the software is universal and helps the species develop its universal physical software during evolution. We as individuals get the universal physical software while we are in our mother's womb. Part of the vital software is personal and is made as we engage in living while we grow up.

Consciousness uses both qualities of creativity and conditioning for building and using the personal software. These qualities are called *guna* in Sanskrit, vital guna to be specific for the vital body. Wrong use of these vital gunas produces defects in the physical body, called *dosha* in Sanskrit, vital dosha to be specific. These doshas play a major role in the healing science of Ayurveda. The way we use the gunas becomes part of our vital character and habit patterns. Note that this character and habits change during each incarnation. Incidentally, quantum theory of reincarnation says that we take these propensities of vital *gunas and doshas* with us from incarnationto incarnation.

As we reach adulthood, our vital body acquires all the personal software needed for the function of the particular physical body. There is the proclivity of conditioning in all of us that tries to maintain status quo. But the biology of consciousness, the science of health demands that we balance creativity and conditioning. It is dynamic equilibrium that a healthy vital-physical body needs. Lack of creativity is what makes the vital body a sheath, a sheath of ignorance.

The Quantum Nature of the Vital Body

Traditional Chinese medicine talks about pathways called *meridians* for the flow of *chi*, the Chinese name for vital energy; the acupuncture points used in Chinese medicine lie along these meridians. If the movement of chi is thus localized, at first sight it may seem that the behaviour of chi is quite Newtonian, deterministic. But East Indians also have mapped the movement of chi which they call *prana* along pathways they call *nadis*, and these nadis do not exactly coincide with the Chinese meridians. This is quite consistent with quantum behaviour--the pathways of neither tradition are concrete, but mere guidelines for intuitive exploration.

So, there must be an uncertainty principle operating between the localization and the direction of movement of chi. This is further confirmed by the fact that the Chinese characterize chi with two complementary aspects of its wholeness (Tao), yin and yang, similar to the complementary characterization of material objects as wave and particle. When we speak of "balancing the vital energy," in Chinese medicine, this means balancing the two polarities of chi.

The journalist Bill Moyer's TV series *Healing and the Mind* for Public Television had a fascinating segment regarding Chinese medicine and the mystery of chi. In one segment, in answer to Moyer's' question, "How does the doctor know he's hitting the right (acupuncture) point?" David Eisenberg, an American apprentice of Chinese medicine, said:

> It's an incredibly difficult thing to do. He asks her whether she feels the chi, and if she has a sensation, that's how he knows. He also has to feel it. My acupuncture teacher said it's like fishing. You must know the difference between a nibble and a bite.

And, of course, it may take years to learn to feel somebody else's chi accurately enough to diagnose malfunction. The feeling of chi is internal, normally not a part of our shared reality. The situation with feelings arising in the brain is a little different; in the brain we have the so-called mirror neurons that evolution has built into us. This gives us the ability to emote somebody else's emotions purely as a local phenomenon. This we experience as sympathy.

In contrast, how the acupuncturist shares in the chi-experience of a patient is like mental telepathy; it works through quantum nonlocality. In what we call empathy, we experience another person's movement of chi at the chakras viscerally in our own experience. An altogether different experience that is accompanied by an expansion of consciousness.

Very good evidence of the quantum nonlocal transfer of chi is coming from controlled experiments in China and elsewhere with *chi gong* (meaning manipulation of chi) masters. These masters of chi-movement are asked to project "good" chi on plants whose metabolic rate of growth is then measured and found to be enhanced. In contrast, when these chi gong masters throw "bad" chi on plants, the plants' metabolic growth rates are found to be adversely affected. Clearly, the experiments show a nonlocal connection between the vital bodies of the chi gong masters with those of the plants. Since nonlocality can never be simulated by

Newtonian machines, this is prime evidence of the quantum nature of the vital body.

II
Scientific Explanation of Chakras and Chakra Psychology

Let's start with what I knew about the chakras in my preparatory exploration on the chakras. I knew that the chakras are seven major places in our body where we feel our major feelings (fig. 17). I also knew that the locations of the chakras are, not coincidentally, at those places where one or more of the major organs of the body are located. Finally, I knew from my own theory that every physical organ has a correlated vital organ, such that, whenever the organ function is called into manifestation, its vital correlate is also brought into manifestation; this movement of the V-organ from possibility to actuality is what we feel as vital energy at the organ site.

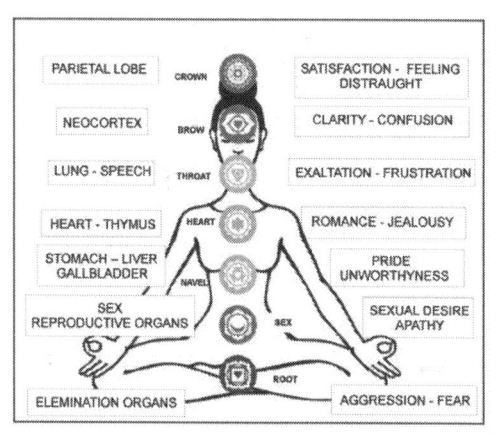

fig. 17: The chakras

Putting all this together, the first insight that came to me was straightforward: chakras are those places along the spine where consciousness collapses an important organ and its vital correlate. For example, take the navel chakra. Here all our digestive organs, the constructive part of metabolism called anabolism, are located – stomach, liver, etc. Indeed, when we eat consciously, these organs come into manifestation along with their V-organs. We feel the movement of vital energy of the V-organ movement. What would be the nature of the feeling? One of security, we are feeding the body nutrition and making it secure. The feeling is also about self-worth, confidence in the body, an identification, a body ego so to speak.

What does yoga psychology based on empirical data say? It agrees with my assessment.

For another example, consider the root chakra, the site of elimination organs. When we pay attention to elimination as elimination happens, the feeling is one of security, all is good. But watch it when we are constipating. We become fearful, reluctant to take risks. Vital energy at the chakra is stuck.

I recently saw a Bollywood movie *Piku* starring the superstar Amitav Bachchan and Deepika Padukone. Amitav played the role of a chronic constipating father; Deepika, the role of his daughter, Piku. Piku has a fiancé. However, when the father and daughter take a trip to Kolkata using a taxi, Piku feels an attraction to the daredevil style of the taxi driver. But of course, being a good girl, she would not possibly give up on his fiancé. Or would she? When the father dies in Kolkata and she returns home, and her fiancé complains about constipating like her father used to do, she hesitated not a moment to break off the relationship and go for a new one with the daredevil albeit reckless taxi driver!

Fear prevents us from love. Besides being an adage of pop psychology, this is also a conclusion of chakra psychology. But how? The explanation required a new insight that took me years to arrive at.

By the way, the heart chakra is the seat of romantic love. Of course! everybody knows that. What everybody does not remember is that the heart's job is to pump blood; this has not much to do with romance. The organ that is relevant is the thymus gland, a part of the immune system. Immune system's job is to distinguish between "me" and "not me," and kill those not-me intruders of the body like bacteria and viruses.

Now imagine you are meeting a person of the opposite sex and he looks and you look and your immune systems (via their V-organs) mutually and non-locally agree to momentarily suspend the immune system function of distinguishing me and not-me. A positive movement, manifestation of the corresponding V- immune, takes place and what would be the feeling associated with this movement? One of "he is mine," right? And of course, reciprocally his feeling would be, "she is mine." This is what we call "romantic love", don't we? Does it not feel wonderful that we now have a scientific explanation of romantic love?

The fifth chakra at the throat, also called throat chakra, is easy to analyse. The organs are organs of expression: speech organs of the brain, the vocal cords, etc. The associated feeling is expressive positive energy. When we are deprived from expressing ourselves, it is common to experience a feeling of being choked at the throat.

The brow chakra, the sixth one, is the chakra associated with thinking. See, the prefrontal cortex is right behind your forehead, and that is where all the rational thinking apparatus lies. Indeed, watch yourself when you engage in serious thinking. You will notice tension at your brow chakra.

The seventh chakra organ is the parietal lobe of the brain, where the capacity of body-image making is located. Every time you pass a mirror and have this irresistible urge to check up on your appearance, don't resist! Your crown chakra is active and healthy.

Fig. 17 shows you a chakra-by-chakra description of the body organs involved and the feelings experienced when 1) the organ is collapsed, call it energy in and 2) the organ stops collapsing, call it energy out.

What is an Emotion? Why are emotions experienced in the brain?

What is an emotion? It is a thought with passion, energy, you say. And you are right. But what kind of energy? This is where it is easy to be confused. Because today almost everybody but the ones like you educated with quantum science interprets energy as physical energy.

It was not always this way. William Blake, a famous eighteenth-century romantic poet, wrote an evocative line in one of his poems, "Energy is eternal delight." But here is a piece of information that should surprise you: the concept of energy came into physics only in circa 1837, not before. So, what energy could Blake be referring to? Obviously vital energy, a nonphysical energy.

The energy of an emotion is energy that you feel—vital energy. An emotion is thought plus feeling. I said before that the job of the mind is to give meaning. More exactly, consciousness uses the mind to give meaning to all its experiences. When consciousness gives meaning to a feeling, the result is an emotional thought, or in short, an emotion.

Why are emotions experienced in the brain? It turns out that evolution has given us instinctual universal software in the form of vital correlates of brain neuronal circuits in an organ in the midbrain called the amygdala and its adjacent areas. When we see a suitable stimulus, this universal software is activated producing response that are referred to as the four F's—fleeing, fighting, feeding, and f-king. These responses are more often than not interpreted by the mind as negative emotions—fleeing corresponds to fear; fighting is response of the negative emotion of anger, violence, competitiveness, or domination; feeding maybe a response to the negative emotion of greed, and f-king to the negative emotion of lust. Notice that for animals without a mind, these instincts are just pure feelings, and are necessities for survival; they are not used in excess. The excessive use of negativity is a contribution of the mind. For animals with mind, for example, chimpanzees and dolphins, we do find emotions and excessive negativity especially when we put them in captivity.

Recent research has also uncovered other interesting data about brain's influence on the body organs. Entire new fields of neuroscientific research—psychoneuroimmunology and psychoneurogastrointestinology--have been created around this new data.

A reasonable hypothesis made by most brain researchers would be that brain takes over the functions of the organs of all the body chakras. This is why they think we never experience pure feelings but always feelings mixed with thoughts—emotions. This is why these people write books on emotions and emotional intelligence entirely based on brain physiology.

But I never gave up on the chakras. And the most recent brain data shows that I was right.

Thanks to experiments at the heart math institute, we now know that when the immune system is suspended, the heart becomes quantum and coherent. In this way love really is quantum energy at the heart.

III
Why fear Suppresses love and love happens when we let go of fear

Back to my research with chakras. I knew that women do make a big deal of experiencing love in their heart implying that they do experience a self-identity there. I even knew that Christian mystics make a big deal of the heart of Jesus. Jesus had an open heart, meaning that he was awakened to the self of the heart. A recent mystic, Ramana Maharshi would swear that there is a self of the heart. I read about that, too.

The discussion in the previous sections leaves the question of the experiencing self at the chakras unanswered. Yes, feelings arise in each of these chakras and they are appropriately connected with the functions of one or more organs in the area of the chakra. But an experience has two poles: subject and object. How does a self-identity arise at each of these chakras? For that, there has to be a tangled hierarchy at a chakra. Are there such tangled hierarchies at each of the chakras?

I knew the question but did not have the answer. So, I remained silent for many years. Perhaps there is no tangled hierarchy and no self-identity at any of the chakras. The potentialities of vital movement can then collapse only in the neocortex with compulsory lacing by thoughts. Perhaps that is why we experience emotions—feelings mixed with thoughts—and not pure feelings, women and mystics notwithstanding.

But this goes against the grain of my own experiences of pure feelings in Richard Moss's workshop that I spoke about earlier and many subsequent experiences. I was also a researcher of creativity that culminated in theory of quantum creativity. During this research I constantly came upon anecdotal data about creative experiences of insight being associated with "gut feeling," and feelings in the heart. I have experienced such feelings myself in connections with my own experiences of creative insight.

Gradually, I became aware of other data that suggested that there might be a self at the heart chakra aside from anecdotal evidence of women talk and mystical literature and creativity research. The new data was objective.

There is now data showing that the immune system has autonomy; I picked up the data in a medical magazine while waiting for the doctor to see me.

Previously, I discussed how romantic love arises from the suspension of immune system function of distinction between me and not me. In this way, episodes of romantic love are periods when the immune system takes a rest. What other system of the body needs such a periodic episode of rest? The neocortex of course. Every night it needs about 8 hours of sleep. Without sleep, brain functions are severely disturbed.

Perhaps it is so for the immune system as well. If the immune system does not get needed occasional rest from love, it malfunctions, does not kill off 'not-me's consisting of abnormal cells thatdivide indefinitely as opposed to normal cells that can divideonly about fifty times. In other words, the malignancy of cancer is produced by a lack of the experience of love in one'slife.

There is an epidemic today, an epidemic of breast cancer in women. Could it be because these women, due to bereavement, suppress love from their regular experience? At Vivekananda Kendra in Bangalore I picked up the news of an Indian Doctor by the name of Chauhan. This doctor used Kirlian photography to measure vital energy blocks in bereaved women's heart chakra and found a positive correlation with incidents of breast cancer.

So, is there a tangled hierarchy at the immune system? A tangled hierarchy exists between an apparatus of perception/cognition and an apparatus for memory. The immune system has the former in the form of feelings, but where is the memory making capacity?

The crucial data came to my awareness a few years ago: yes, there has been a big breakthrough in brain research, the discovery of a big bundle of nerves at the heart chakra—memory-making capacity. Conclusion: There is a tangled hierarchy in the immune system giving it a self of the heart and the autonomy that comes with it.

The autonomy is somewhat compromised by the psychoneuroimmunological connection with the brain. So, we have to own up to the self of the heart, a process that takes some practice.

Another big bundle of nerves has been discovered also at the navel chakra. Like the heart, the navel chakra also has a self. The potentialities of vital feeling can manifest at the heart, at the navel, and of course, at the brain's neocortex, brow chakra.

But there is no self at the root chakra and the sex chakra. When we are not aware of feelings in the body, when the self-experiences at the navel and the heart are suppressed, the energies at the root chakra (and the sex chakra) cannot collapse at those chakras. But what happens when we become aware?

With awareness regained at the navel chakra, we can collapse the uncollapsed root chakra vital energy at the navel. How do we experience that? As courage. Goodbye anal retentivity. This is an example of vital creativity.

Furthermore, when the heart chakra opens in this creative way, we can even allow the root chakra potentialities to rise all the way up to the heart before collapsing them. Letting go of fear and opening the heart for love. Are you ready for vital creativity?

IV
The Male-Female Difference

Cultures all over the world have always insisted about the necessity of women keeping their heart awareness by encouraging them from childhood to love others even at the expense of not loving themselves.

Not loving yourself suppresses the navel self. The biological function here is anabolism—the positive side of metabolism. When the navel chakra is part open, the feelings associated for excess energy are pride and narcissism. For deficit of attention, the feeling is unworthiness. When fully open, the feeling at the chakra is one of self-respect and self-worth. Old Eastern cultures, therefore, put much value to this chakra and its cultivation (unfortunately only for men). In Japan, it is recognized as the site of the body-ego--*hara*. The word *hara-kiri* meaning suicide originated from this connotation.

When the brain and the mind enter the picture, the corresponding instinctual brain circuit dominates behaviour, and the ego-self that we identify with is the mental ego. The feelings at the navel chakra likewise become part of our unconscious suppression-repression dynamic.

When an unconscious feeling of unworthiness surfaces via its effect on other conscious feelings what happens? There are two poles of possible behaviour: one is to continue to hide the feeling and behave like a narcissistic diva, as self-centred as can be. The other pole of behaviour is to try to please the other, to prove your worthiness to him/her.

Here is a culturally encouraged female-male difference: the females are encouraged in most cultures to be pleasers, males to act as narcissistic. Many males add to their narcissism through the use of their sexuality for sexual conquests. They learn to use sex to boost their body ego. Some men become sexual predators. Other males recover some of their self-worth through masturbation.

Most cultures do not allow the females to be promiscuous; so, most females never recover from their habits of pleasing others. In fact, they become more and more dependent on others for the vicarious feeling of worthiness. They become needy.

Some of the female divas do use sexuality to boost the body-ego. They are the independent women even in traditional societies.

This entire dynamic changes when you, the female, cultivate body-awareness and appreciate visceral feelings and your navel chakra opens more. Now you pay attention to the energies in the navel and cultivate self-worth. No longer do you need to please compulsively; nor do you need to hide your unworthiness behind the veil of a diva. Most of all, opening and cultivating this chakra is a necessary ingredient for becoming independent and eventually an original individual.

For males, it is equally imperative to develop a more open heart by cultivating other love. Remember, you can love yourself only to the extent you understand what love is—that love begins with the ability to include another in your consciousness—other love.

Chapter 5
Discovering the Third Layer of Reality: Mind with Meaning

I
What is Mind?

What is mind? Nobody quite knew in the modern scientific era. When you don't know, you can joke about it. A neuroscientist, a Nobelist John Eccles, when asked, *What is mind?* said, "Doesn't matter." When the questioner asked the follow-up question, "What is matter?" Eccles said, "Never mind," playing a clever pun.

Did the boy in the Upanishadic story in chapter 1 know what mind is? We must assume he did; otherwise how could he propose that reality is mind? But the Upanishads do not clarify, present day mystics have to wing it, and they fail miserably.

In 1995, the Vivekananda Kendra in Bangalore arranged a series of debates between me and the local spiritual teacher, no names please. When he tried to explain how consciousness involutes into matter, he said, "Just as vapor condenses into liquid condenses into solid, consciousness in the form of anandamaya kosha--progressively condenses into the Vigynamaya kosha, to monomaya kosha, to pranamaya kosha, to matter."

When my turn came to speak, I politely pointed out that mind (*manas* in Sanskrit), vital energy (*prana*), the material, they each belong to a different logical category, impossible to convert from one to the other. The poverty of this kind of conceptualization becomes clear with scientific thinking. Matter is hardware with hardware laws. One such law is the law of conservation of baryon number—the total number of baryons in the material world remains a constant in all transactions. What is a baryon? They are the heavy part of the submicroscopic constituents of matter, objects like protons and neutrons; the light part goes by the name of lepton such as electrons.

If mind or vital energy could be changed into matter, the number of baryons in the material world would get a boost that is not allowed by the laws of science, quantum science included.

To his credit, the spiritual teacher did not hesitate to change his mind upon hearing my scientific explanation of what vital energy consists of (see chapter 4), what mind must consist of (see below).

First, we create new vocabulary. There is a tendency in the literature to use the word mind with the meaning "consciousness." We are not going to do that. For us, mind is the vehicle consciousness uses for thought--the objects of meaning.

Most brain scientists look at the brain as a computer with a mind of its own, not separate from it. But thought has meaning and you know you can use your computer to make software of *your* mental meaning. See the problem? As far as you know, computers cannot process meaning by itself, only what you give it. There is now quite a convincing proof of this that I will discuss later. Is your mind similarly separate from your brain? It certainly does not resemble the brain or anything physical experientially.

Is mind nonphysical? If so, how does it interact with the brain which is physical? They have nothing in common; they need a mediator, but where is the mediator? So, scientists in the main avoid this dualism of mind and brain and think mind is a creation of the brain.

But then too, the thorny question, *Can the brain process meaning?* It certainly can process what is programmed into it— old meaning. Then the question is, *How did the old meaning get there? From other people? True, but how did it get into the first person who thought it?* And of course, we ourselves have new thoughts that have new meaning, as for example, creative thought. Many brain scientists deny creativity to fit the brain to their thinking. Would you like to see yourself as incapable of creativity?

I think it is the opposite; you would like to know how to enhance your creativity, and how to optimize your mental function of creativity.

I think, and I call the thinking, part of my mind. One author gave a wonderful list of relevant questions about the mind that I copied down but forgot to write down the reference. I will use these questions one by one as the springboard for a discussion.

Is the "mind" something different from the "brain"? If it is, then what is the relationship between the two, and how, when and why this relationship takes place?

Descartes thought mind is different from the brain; it is nonphysical. In his time and until recently this philosophy of dualism, was not considered scientific because of the naughty question, *How does the mind interact with the brain?* If the interaction is via signals, as material interactions are, then there is a problem. Signals carry energy; but energy is always a constant for the physical world alone.

In the quantum paradigm, the dualism problem has been solved. There is signalless communication; we call it nonlocality. So nonphysical mind and physical brain can communicate through nonlocality, through consciousness.

Is "thought" responsible for the creation of the "self", or the "I", or the "me"? For example, Descartes said, I think, therefore I am. Is there validity in this statement?

Up till recently, Descartes' statement *I think therefore I am* has produced another knot in Western philosophical thinking that consciousness is the creation of the mind, it is part of the mind. The quantum paradigm enables us to think differently:

mind, like matter, is a compartment of consciousness, consisting of potentialities of meaning. In this way, in quantum thinking it is consciousness, not mind, that observes, that thinks. In this way, what used to be called the mind-brain problem has also been solved.

Are those "structures" the initial point from where one "thinks" that one "observes"? Is an "observation" the result of the activity of "thought"? If it is, therefore there is no observation at all, there is only "thought"!

Both observation (perception) and thought are activities of consciousness. No, observation is not the result of the activity of thought as Bishop Berkeley posited in the eighteenth century. Mind helps consciousness to give meaning to all our experiences in the form of thought. Perception plus thought is cognition. But thought is not the only means of cognition by any means. There is also feelings.

Is the "brain" the result of the accumulation of knowledge, what becomes "memory"? Therefore, is the "brain" limited to its own content (memory)?

How is this content (memory) of the "brain" accessed? Is the access of the "brain" to its own content (memory) what we call "thought"?

The brain makes a neuronal representation of mental meaning mind gives the physical (and all other) experience; this is sometimes called a memory engram. Once the brain has it, exciting it will automatically play back the mind-interpreted event in the correlated mind; that is the gist of their joint act. There is no doubt about it. Memory is brain-mind memory; mind and brain work together to make memory.

Can we directly prove that memory has a mental quantum component? Yes, we can. We have. The psychologist Tony Marcel's cognitive data with perception of ambiguous words looks anomalous until you realize that memory has a mental component and it is quantum (see later).

If the brain were a computer acting alone, the question of retrieval is difficult, no buttons to push.

How do we retrieve memory? Via intention. In the quantum model, memory is potentiality of consciousness and consciousness retrieves it via choice. Our intention signals nonlocal consciousness to choose and actualize the memory we desire.

Is there an action that does not come from the content of the "brain" (memory)?

Does thought only result from existing brain-mind memory? The answer here is crucial. According to scientific materialism, it does. The new science explored in this book says, no. We have creativity, ability of creative thinking that breaks away from the past memory.

Is it possible to get in touch with something that is actual, without depending on the idea of "time" what so ever?

Let's dig deeper into the nature of the brain-mind's dual partnership. The part of the brain that helps make memory is a computer; it processes symbols, information. Mind provides the meaning which the brain represents as symbol; the meaning then becomes information. Creativity is the discovery of new meaning.

Is it possible to get in touch with something actual, in a timeless way? Yes, it is. In the new science creativity leads us to discover things in their suchness, not tainted by time and memory. (One way) time is created by memory.

II
Is Mind Brain?

The scientific materialist view is to keep things parsimonious. Do we really need a nonphysical mind? Can we not assume mind is brain? Certainly, thoughts arise in us always in conjunction with the brain. Why not assume that brain is the cause of the mental thought?

So again, Is mind brain? Let's examine this from a modern kid's point of view who has a cell phone and a laptop with free access to social media both of which he or she uses aplenty to keep boredom away.

What do these young people process? They process information—other people's meanings. They never bother about their own meaning about anything.

I already mentioned the work of the philosopher John Searle about how computers cannot process meaning. Searle set up a thought experiment as follows. Imagine you bring a Chinese story to be translated by a Chinese room of artificial intelligence machines, computers. A robot picks up your Chinese story and puts it into Chinese machine symbols that are now mechanically translated into English symbols by the Chinese room translating machine. The output gets to another robot that changes the English computer symbols into English language output for a human client like you. This is how a Google translator works.

Searle's point is that nowhere in the steps of this procedure is any understanding involved. Symbols processing symbols is what a machine does, no understanding. Understanding is left to humans.

But today young humans don't try to understand things either. They are happy with processing information for information's sake; anything to keep away from boredom! Effectively, today's young people are using the brain in a machine-like way. Ask them! They are happy like never before. No boredom!

"But you said what the young people process as information originated as meaning that other people processed," you can complain. "So, somebody somewhere is processing meaning."

Is there? Suppose these people's meanings also derive from other people's meaning via a process called logical or rational thinking. Via algorithms like those that computers use. How are these people different from robots then?

Suppose there never is any new meaning! Just as evolution proceeds via genes that evolve via chance mutation and natural selection, similarly there are "memes" of the mind—basic mental information—that propagate through evolution in a similar way. All mental meaning is nothing but the propagation of the selfish meme driven by survival necessity!

Let's consider a simple model of memes—the English letters of the alphabet. And then think about how Einstein may have discovered his famous law $E = mc^2$. The famous cartoonist Sydney Harris did a caricature of this. Einstein writes on a black board, $E = ma^2$, shakes his head and crosses it out and writes $E = mb^2$ and crosses that out also. The caption says, *The Creative moment.*

Is a creative moment like this? For algorithmic creativity, it is. But is real creativity like this? Why are you laughing giving away that you don't believe so? Would a teenager who grows up today with information processing alone see the joke?

Many scientists still think creativity is humbug, new meaning is humbug, it is just recycling permutations and combinations of old meanings. Many scientists still believe, all science is discovered by using the scientific method of "try it and see".

Searle's point is that computers cannot process meaning starting from scratch; in other words, new meaning. This is the point. *Is there new meaning or not?*

Quantum science gives an affirmative answer to the question of new meaning. New meaning comes from previously un-collapsed possibilities of meaning in the unconscious. But even so, could this new meaning be permutations and combination of old meanings?

The definitive argument comes when we include the archetypes in our argument. Archetypes cannot be directly represented in our physical hardware. So, if you discover a new meaning in a new archetypal context, there is your evidence of a discovery of new meaning that will mute the hard sceptic. I call such discoveries fundamental creativity. In contrast, creativity staying within known contexts is situational creativity.

Einstein's discovery of the equivalence of mass and energy $E = mc^2$ changed the scientific law of macro material movement from Newtonian to Einsteinian, relativistic, although in the limit of small velocities, we get by with the simpler Newton's laws of motion. This is fundamental creativity at its best.

Does one have to engage in Fundamental Creativity of Einsteinian Genius to Discover the Mind then?

Fortunately, no. Einstein's discovery above was a discovery of outer creativity. There is also inner creativity, I change my self, my ego, every time I go the process of understanding somebody else's meaning. Searle, too, makes this point.

Translation, mostly, can be done mechanically, without understanding. Then it is information processing. But if even today's teenagers try to understand the meaning of a message—somebody else's meaning—in his or her own way—that would be a human activity; no machine could do it because it is subjective.

Mind you. Understanding is different from seeing that somebody's message is logical from the point of view of your own internal logic. Understanding happens when you incorporate somebody's meaning by a quantum change—a discontinuous change—in your previous belief system. This is what today's teenagers do not do. And this is why we say that they are dumbing themselves down.

By the time one becomes an adult, the brain has all the mental memory—that is, mental software—to carry out its mental functions. The entire collection of mental software is our mental body. Mental health demands that we keep the mental body in a dynamic state via a balanced use of creativity and conditioning, our mental gunas.

III
The Quantum Nature of the Mind

Mind processes meaning, but is the processing quantum? The physicist David Bohm showed how you could experience the quantum nature of thought directly.

Material quantum objects obey the uncertainty principle--we cannot simultaneously measure both their position and velocity with utmost accuracy. In order to determine the trajectory of an object, we need to know not only where an object is now but also where it will be a little later; in other words, both its position and velocity, simultaneously. So, we can never determine accurate trajectories of material quantum objects.

Bohm pointed out that an uncertainty principle operates also for thoughts. If we focus on the content of thought as when we meditate on a mantra, we lose the direction which the thought is following. On the other hand, focusing on the direction of thought as when we are on a psychiatrist's sofa free-associating, leads to a loss of its content. Try it and see. The content of the thought is called its feature; the line of thought is the thought's association.

So, Bohm's observation (and yours, if you have tried the little experiment) reveals only one thing: a thought is a quantum object that appears and moves in the field of our internal awareness just as physical objects appear and move in ordinary space.

But thoughts appear in awareness only when we are actually thinking. Where does a thought go between our measurements, between thinking? It spreads as a wave of possibilities of meaning, what else? Exactly like material quantum objects, thought exists in consciousness as transcendent potentiality of many possible meanings; collapse manifests them in awareness in a form described by complementary attributes such as feature and association.

The quantum picture forces us to think about the physical and mental worlds differently from how we are used to thinking of them. Normally, we think of both these worlds as made of substances. Sure, the mental substance is subtle, we cannot quantify it in the same way as we can the physical, but it is still a substance, or so we think. We need to change this view. Even the physical is not substance in the ordinary sense, let alone the mental. Both physical and mental worlds remain as possibilities until consciousness gives them substantiality by collapsing an actual experience.

But there are differences between physical and mental substances when we experience them. One big difference is the grossness, externality of the macro world of our shared perception of the physical domain. In comparison, the mental world is experienced as subtle, internal.

As Descartes correctly intuited, mental substance is indivisible. For this substance, then, there is no reduction to smaller and smaller, there is no micro out of which the macro is made. So, the mental world is considered whole, one that physicists sometimes call an infinite medium. There can be waves in such infinite media, modes of movement that can only be described as quantum possibility waves. And we directly observe (collapse) these quantum modes without the intermediary of the macro mental measurement apparatus (there isn't any). But we pay a price. In between collapses and experiences, the mental modes are subject to rapid quantummovement; they quickly expand and become large pools of possible meanings. What this means is that between my collapse and your collapse, between my thinking and your thinking, the quantum mental modes would have expanded in possibility so much that it becomes unlikely that you willcollapse the same thought as me. Therefore, two different people cannot ordinarily share thoughts; thoughts are private, they are experienced internally.

This internality is positive proof, that mind is quantum and its arena is infinite with no micro-macro division. Moreover, by the same token of internality, we can safely assume that the vital world of feeling and the supramental world of intuition are also quantum worlds.

There is another way all these worlds clearly show evidence of their quantum nature: they are nonlocal and discontinuous, very quantum-like, in their operation. Nonlocality of the mind is revealed in such phenomenon as mental telepathy and distant viewing; discontinuity is revealed in the phenomenon of creativity in which we discover new meaning of value. Nonlocality is signal-less communication, but what is discontinuity? As mentioned before, when electrons jump from one atomic orbit to another, they never go through the intermediate space; the electron's jump is a quantum leap. Similarly, when we experience a creative insight, the experience is sudden—discontinuous--without intermediate steps of reasoned algorithms. The signature of a creative insight's discontinuity is the surprise; the reason creative experiences are called "aha" experiences in the literature.

A reminder. However, when all is said and done, realize that only the material world has memory making capacity; thus, only the material world can give us a tangled hierarchy, which is why the material world is essential for manifestation. No wonder the wisdom traditions in India call the human birth in a material body a very precious thing.

IV
Are Thoughts Possibilities of Meaning before We Experience them? Marcel's Experiment

I now want to discuss an experiment that brilliantly illustrates both the quantum possibility wave aspect of the processing of meaning by the mind as well as the efficacy of the quantum actualization model to distinguish between the unconscious and the conscious.

The original purpose of the psychologist Tony Marcel's experiment in 1980 was to use words with ambiguous meaning in a series of three words to check the congruence or incongruence of meaning. He measured the subject's reaction time as an indicator of the relationship between the words in such strings as hand-palm-wrist (congruent), tree-palm-wrist (incongruent), clock-palm-wrist (unbiased), and clock-ball-wrist (unassociated). His subjects watched a screen on which the three words of the series were flashed one by one with an interval of either 600 milliseconds or 1.5 seconds between them. For example, the flash of the word hand before the flashing of the word palm should bias the hand meaning of palm that then should lead to an improvement of the subject's reaction time to recognize wrist. This is congruence. For incongruence as in the string tree-palm-wrist, the biasing word tree should inspire the tree meaning of the word palm thus leading to an increased reaction time for recognizing the third word wrist. And indeed, this is what was found to be the case.

There is a trick called "masking" that advertisers use a lot to present sexy subliminal messages to attract the attention of the viewer. The viewer processes the subliminal message unconsciously. So, masking a word by a pattern, would force a viewer to process the word unconsciously although consciously he or she could not see it.

In Marcel's experiment, when the middle word was masked by a pattern, there was no appreciable difference between the reaction times between the congruent and incongruent cases. As I said above, pattern masking prevents conscious processing but allows unconscious processing. What the experiment proves then is that in unconscious processing, both of the possible meanings of the ambiguous word palm remain accessible, no collapse and no choice, and therefore, no biasing of any meaning and the difference between the congruent and incongruent situation disappears.

I will spare you the detailed analysis, but this experiment defies alternative models of explanation. The conclusions of this experiment are unambiguous: 1) mind is quantum; and 2) the quantum model for the distinction of the unconscious and the conscious is the right model.

V
Zen Mind, Quantum Physics, and Creativity

Zen is one way to get into the puzzles of quantum physics by way of the mind. But first a confession: this chapter has some overlap with a similar chapter in my book *The Everything Answer Book*.

In Zen, they talk about two domains of reality—the domain of emptiness and the domain of form. As in the koan: "What is your name before you were born?" This idea of two domains of reality is the very same as the quantum idea of two domains—potentiality and actuality—that we introduce in connection with the wave-particle duality. Also, consciousness enters into the affairs of the two realms in quantum physics as in Zen. For example, the Zen story: Two monks were arguing. One was saying, "The flag is moving." The other was saying, "No, the wind is moving." A master was passing by. He admonished, "The flag is not moving; the wind is not moving. Your consciousness is moving."

If you look at Zen koans, or Zen stories like the one above, you are puzzled in the same way that a student, when he or she is first introduced to quantum physics, is puzzled; indeed, the physicist Niels Bohr used to say, "If you are not puzzled by quantum physics, you couldn't possibly have understood it." Of course, puzzling alone may not be enough for getting to the meaning of quantum physics. You really have to include consciousness and the meaning-giving mind in the exploration of your quantum puzzle to breakthrough into the meaning of quantum physics.

See it is like this. If you ask a chemistry professor, "Professor how do you know so much?" the professor will likely say, "Because I open my eyes." But if you ask a Zen Master, "Master, how do you know so much?" the master will say, "Because I close my eyes."

Do you get it? If your worldview is based on opening your eyes, you look at material objects at the macro level, and that fits Newtonian worldview. That gives you a belief system. The Macro world is approximately Newtonian. With that prejudice, the message of the micro world of quantum weirdness can be compromised because you believe that it has no tangible effect on the macro world of your experience.

There is a Zen story that warns us of this possibility. A science professor has come to visit a Zen master. He is all eager to talk. The Master says, "Let's have some tea," and goes to the kitchen to make tea. The professor follows him and starts giving him an earful about his own knowledge of Zen, bla…bla…bla. The tea is made. The professor sits down on the table and keeps talking. The Zen master also keeps pouring the tea in the professor's cup. Of course, the cup overflows. The professor shouts, "Stop, stop, don't you see the cup is already full?" The Zen master stops as he looks at the professor, "So is you mind about what you think Zen is. How can I teach when your mind is already full?"

If on the other hand, your conceptualization of reality—your worldview—is based upon closing your eyes and the experiences of the internal world, you are looking at the world from layers 2 and 3, maybe even 4 and 5. That's where consciousness shows up in your experience; that's where the quantum and the subtle show up.

It is like this in Zen, the puzzle is about the quantum movement of the subtle and the sense of wonder it brings. Sometimes the master would say something that sounds totally obscure, totally nonsensical, and yet there is wisdom in pursuing it and seeing what the meaning is—in terms of a creative awakening in the person who is solving the koan. I suggest that you take a similar approach to initiate yourself in quantum physics. It's not a bunch of information. Instead, if we discover the deeper meaning of the new information being presented, we find that it gives us an awakening into the nature of reality itself.

In the Zen way of thinking, opposites can exist at the same time; contradictory things can exist at the same time, in consciousness. For example, there is this story. A master was teaching two disciples; a third one sitting a little further away was witnessing. At one point, one disciple expressed his understanding of what the master was teaching. The master said, "Yes, you are right." The other disciple in his turn gives a completely different interpretation of the master's teaching. The master said, "You are right." Both students went away satisfied. The witnessing guy however got irate, "Master, you are getting old. How can they both be right? The master looked at him and said, "You, too, are right."

Quantum physics seems to work in a similar way. To a proposition, the opposite proposition could be also true. Like the proposition, a quantum object is a wave. It is true indeed. Its opposite proposition, a quantum object is a particle, is also true, however. So, in quantum physics from the get-go, we have this opposition of concepts being forced upon us by the nature of objects. We should not take the opposition to be literally true. It is an invitation to go deeper.

You know in the world of psychotherapy, we often talk about double-bind/double-mind, like when you want to do something but you cannot because you are stuck in the double bind. Also, in the everyday reality we keep facing contradictory options. We want to decide, but we cannot because we want to keep all options open. So, this way of thinking that we could keep all options open at the same time in potentiality could be helpful both in the world of therapy and in the worlds of everyday life.

In psychotherapy, the domain of potentiality that can contain exclusive options at the same time is called the unconscious. More and more psychotherapists are realizing the value of unconscious processing in therapy. Similarly, if people allow the unconscious to process their choices, they would do better off.

But we are going a little bit ahead of ourselves. So, let's go slowly and see how we get into these ideas that are very useful in psychotherapy and in ordinary life or in creativity, in our search for truth itself. Take this juxtaposition of opposites. The important thing to recognize from the beginning is that in quantum physics, it's built into the nature of reality. In psychology or in creativity, in order to get a breakthrough, psychologists sometimes artificially create an oppositional situation and process it in the unconscious to get new results. When quantum physics says an object is both wave and particle, it's not a teaching tool or a tool to jump beyond both. It is really the case.

In this way, when the new science posits that meaning is a quantum object, meaning naturally takes on many facets, including opposites in the unconscious. It is not an artifice. Metaphors, polysemous words, abstract paintings, create multiple meanings deliberately, but in truth, any word, any object can evoke multiple meanings in the unconscious.

Be curious. Think about this domain beyond time and space. Is it similar to consciousness? Is it the real domain of consciousness? And realize this: this domain is not only like consciousness; this domain *is* consciousness. The breakthrough idea came soon after experimental data showed that there is a way to experimentally discern between the domain of potentiality, where objects are waves of possibility, and the domain of actuality in which objects are particle. I referred to Aspect's experiment before. Alain Aspect, a French physicist and his collaborators created this experiment to prove that this domain of potentiality has a unique, defining characteristic. Communications in this domain potentially do not require any signals, once objects interact locally and activate their oneness. What this means is astounding. Communication is instantaneous basically means that this domain is potentially just one thing. All objects in it are potentially one interconnected stuff.

In other words, like right now we are communicating through words; I have written some words, and you are reading them using signals in space and time. But we can also use this domain of potentiality, you know. If I have a strand of thought but I am not saying it verbally or in the words of a book, that thought could be spreading via the domain of potentiality and reaching you. Instantly. Can that happen? Yes, it can; it does happen. That is when we are inspired by an author's words or imagery; the words act as a trigger of the nonlocal connection.

With this understanding, let's go into Zen. In Zen Buddhism, we find riddles like this. "What is the sound of one hand clapping?" "What is your name before you were born?" What this is referring to is this very idea that things are born out of a potentiality. The thought was a potentiality of many meanings before it became an actual thought with one unique meaning. And in that potentiality, the possibility wave of thought has many facets. The conversion of potentiality into actuality converts a many-faceted object into a one-faceted object, wave into a particle.

Most of us tend to think that consciousness exists because there are human beings, but according to this book, it sounds like consciousness is already there whether human beings are there or not. Consciousness already exists as the ground of the domain of potentiality.

That is the point. But remember, this domain manifests, so we find that the manifestation of consciousness as self-awareness happens at the same time as objects convert from waves into particles.

In this domain of potentiality, there is no form yet, but form is manifested into a specific way in the domain of actuality. So, if we know the key of how to manifest form in the specific way we want or need in this space-time domain, then we would be able to use this key to solve problems, or we would be able to manifest what we want in this reality. But we need some capability to influence whatever it is in that potentiality domain.

The meanings that we think in this domain of actuality become possibilities for processing in that domain of potentiality. The poet Wallace Stevens wrote:

> They said, you have a blue guitar
> You don't play things as they are.
> The man said, "Things as they are
> Are changed on my blue guitar."

Consciousness with its blue guitar of quantum science and its laws changes the meanings we consciously process into many possible meanings. If we feed ambiguity, conflicted meaning, we generate ever more possibilities for the unconscious to chew on.

In this way, we influence the domain of potentiality to proliferate into many possibilities. That gives us an opportunity of simultaneously processing all these various possibilities and their combination, an entire gestalt, that are available for getting an answer to the problem at hand.

This is where Zen and quantum physics become the same kind of approach to the human consciousness and mind. Both Zen thinking and quantum thinking is based on allowing two levels of thinking. In contrast, you can think about machine thinking or Newtonian thinking or ordinary thinking as one-level thinking. In one-level thinking, in manifest space-time what we call conscious thinking, we can look at various possible answers, but only one answer at a time. But as I said, when we allow the processing not only in the space-time domain but also in the domain of potentiality, then we can process many possible answers at the same time, as a wave of all the possibilities. The space-time domain is good for processing a whole bunch of divergent answers one by one; we call it divergent thinking. But to converge to the gestalt of a solution, convergent thinking, simultaneous processing of many possibilities in the domain of potentiality is so much more effective. Except that we have to acknowledge that the processing is very different in the domain of potentiality. In space-time, we are conscious; in the domain of potentiality we are unconscious. Only after repeated bouts of conscious and unconscious processing --do-be-do-be-do-- does convergent thinking manifest in the form of a quantum leap.

Einstein said this about the efficacy of unconscious processing: "I think 99 times and find nothing. I stop thinking, swim in the silence, and the truth comes to me."

One important question: If quantum potentiality can contain multiple possibilities for what we are seeking, there are possibilities for getting things better and also possibilities for things to get worse. And of course, we want things to get better, so how could we retrieve the particular possibility of getting things better amidst all the potentiality?

This is a very good question. We cannot guarantee. Obviously then, our creative insights to a problem can give others very painful consequences. No Japanese person needs to be reminded of the pain that the atomic bomb brought into the world. And yet the scientists who developed the atomic bomb certainly used quantum thinking and Zen thinking.

What I am saying is exactly true in our personal life too. For instance, we enter into situations where we become very obtuse about how or whether to make quantum changes. But these are the times when we need the breakthrough and reach the next stage of personal growth.

The following Zen story used to bother me a lot. A student, a young boy was mocking his Zen master. The Zen master had a habit that the boy would imitate; the habit was to hold up his forefinger, so the boy did that too. One day, the boy held up his forefinger again in imitation, and the Zen master witnessed the act. He seized the boy and, using a sharp knife, chopped off the offending finger. When the boy cried out in agony, the Zen master called out the boy's name to gain his attention and raised up his forefinger. The story goes that the boy was enlightened in that moment. He needed a jolt. It took me a long time to realize that what seems like an evil is sometimes necessary because we are so "dumb," that unless we suffer, we don't quantum jump into the reality.

Some people have to invite cancer into their body, a dreadful disease. And we can feel sorry for him or her. That's one response. We can also think of it as consciousness using a two-by-four to hit us with, so we can wake up. It gives us an opportunity to use quantum healing, which is a quantum leap in emotional thought that heals cancer by correcting the result of faulty meaning processing (of feelings) and restoring the immune system in full health. If one is ready, the same quantum leap can be a quantum leap to "enlightenment."

In the Zen tradition, one has to go through five days of very strenuous meditation, which gives a lot of pain to the knees and temporarily, you lose focus, and your mind wanders. But after you have done that for quite a few times, you learn to relax when pain comes. The result is alternate doing and being—focused attention and relaxation, do-be-do-be-do. Then you go into the master's room, and the master looks at you. All of a sudden, you have this satori, a quantum leap.

The Zen way of reaching sudden enlightenment was shrouded with mystery for a long time. The mystery is solved when we consider the quantum process of creativity; do-be-do-be-do *that* is the fundamental mystery of creativity. Creativity is work, according to most people. This, the creativity field researchers find, is ironically not quite true. Of course, when we first started in science, then many people, many scientists, thought that all creative ideas are discovered because of the clever use of the so-called scientific method – *Try it and see*, and they tried to glamorize the idea that because scientists *try* and *see*, that verification is the crucial approach to creativity. Pretty soon the researchers found that this would be a very inefficient way of finding answers to really difficult and ambiguous questions, because there are just too many possibilities to "try and see" individually. It would take much, much more than lifetimes and lifetimes of individual people. Was there a better way? And then they looked and looked at many, many case histories. They always found that researchers, even in science, work very hard to explore the problem, find some answers, existing hints, and then they just relax. Just relax. Do nothing, and often their ideas spring up from that relaxed state. A Zen poem:

> Sitting quietly, doing nothing
> The spring comes; and the grass grows by itself [in spurts].

I have a Japanese friend who was a copywriter in an advertising firm for a while in his youth. His colleagues were more or less laid back, easy-going people. Some of them had bottles of whiskey in a drawer, and some of them would say, "Oh it's such a good day. Let's go to Mt. Fuji!" But he discovered that those seemingly easy-going, laidback people also had lots of playfulness and seemed to be able to explore creativity much better than busy-busy-busy uptight people.

That's the message of creativity field research. Creativity not only requires the focus of driving intensity, which most people do have today, but also requires the relaxed being. Do and be. These are the first two stages of the creative process: Preparation and unconscious processing.

For quite a while, this was well known but there was no explanation of this. When quantum physics and its proper consciousness-based interpretation came along, I found the explanation very easily. In between the events of choice, quantum objects being possibility waves, they spread. If you throw a pebble in the water, the water waves expand, right? So, the same thing happens with quantum waves of possibility. They literally expand and become bigger and bigger pools of possibility for you to choose from. So obviously there is advantage in waiting and not thinking, thinking, thinking, because if you choose very fast, the pool of possibility you choose from will be small, whereas if you wait, that pool of possibilities will be considerably bigger, and that obviously has tremendous advantage for your creativity.

This is what creative people do, and then there is a little bit of addition to that, which is that if you wait too long, then you simply lose your focus on your problem; there also has to be that sense of urgency that takes us to creative insights.

My Japanese copywriter friend I mentioned before told me this. After he graduated from the university, he worked at an advertising agency for about 15 years. In advertising, there is always a deadline for the copywriter to create catchwords or catch phrases. Never was there a time when the idea and inspiration did not come to him before the deadline. And he was amazed because it always came. Today, when I teach students transformational courses that require term papers, I give them deadlines. And I always encourage them to prepare and relax but never write the final version until the deadline is close.

So again, it's not a wise thing to lose focus entirely and become too addicted to being. Neither strategy, too much doing and too much being, is a good idea. What you need to do is alternative being and doing. This is what I call jokingly do-be-do-be-do, borrowing from the Frank Sinatra jingle.

How did I come up with the idea of do-be-do-be-do? Creativity researchers usually say that creativity consists of four consecutive stages: preparation, unconscious processing, sudden insight, and manifestation of the product. I thought there was something missing here but could not figure out what.

I spoke of a Sydney Harris cartoon of Einstein's discovery of $E = mc^2$ before. My friend the artist Terry Way did a cartoon of my discovery of do-be-do-be-do in the same spirit (fig. 18). But of course, it did not happen that way.

fig. 18

The Creative Moment, after a cartoon by Sidney Harris

One night, I had a dream. In the dream, there was a stage and some stick figures came along and started dancing, gambolling, a lot of activity. A voice in the background said, "These are the angels of doing." After a while, they went away and were soon followed by another bunch of stick figures. But these figures just sat and meditated, doing nothing. The voice in the background said, "These are the angels of being." Then they went away and were replaced by the angels of doing. And then they went away and the angels of being came back. And so on and so forth it went. When I woke up, I had the quantum leap about the missing item in the creative process. I thought of the jingle, do-be-do-be-do.

I really think the idea of a quantum leap for solving problems is very important, and we should attempt to utilize it in the three-dimensional space-time reality where we live whenever we can. For physical and mental health, we are already using it with considerable success. Why can't we use it in business, in politics, in resolving conflicts? And you know, the general wisdom is, people are more or less logical, in their *head* so to speak. But in truth, this is only true of men if that. Women, who by the way are seventy percent of the quantum activists in the world right now, are quite different. They are open to higher emotions; they are in their *heart* at least some of the time. When we integrate the head and the heart, reason and emotions, we transcend both. With quantum creativity we then can resolve conflicts easily without going into war.

As we try to make a quantum leap into the new reality, which element is more needed – rational elements or non-rational elements as emotions and intuitions? Do we need to focus more on feeling and intuition or focus on the mental, logical? Neither exclusively, what we need is a combination of both. You have to remember it is the West where Japanese Zen and Indian yoga flourished just as these practices were waning in Japan and India. And indeed, today there are a lot of Zen and yoga aficionados in the West, that way of thinking where we create a cloud of unknowing before we get to take the quantum leap to wisdom is catching on in the Western culture. Acknowledging this cloud of unknowing is an endeavour where indeed intuitions and emotions must enter, must guide us. They play a very important role. Intuitions and emotions are not continuously study-able through any kind of step-by-step procedure that we call rationality. So, in that sense, in the creative process, there is a component where emotions and intuitions play a huge role. Yet there is also a component where we have to focus; we have to bring conscious rational effort into the process of creativity. And that's why the idea of very rational focusing as well as letting go is simultaneously important as in awareness meditation.

This reminds me of a Zen story. A student has finished fourteen years of awareness training. So, his Zen master has invited him to his house for a celebratory dinner. It is a rainy day. As the fellow arrives, he puts down his umbrella, then takes off his shoes and goes inside. The master welcomes him and then asks, "Did you bring an umbrella?"

"Yes, Master, I did," says our student.

"You also took off your shoes outside I see. Very thoughtful."

"Thank you, Master."

"Now tell me, which side of the umbrella did you leave your shoes; on the left or on the right?"

Alas! The fellow does not remember. "Master, I am not aware," he says. "Well, fourteen more years of awareness training for you," says the master.

Chapter 6

Try to Create the Inner Reality You Like and Live there or Integrate the Inner and the Outer? Schizophrenia, Drugs, and Dreams

I
Brain in Transition

In February 2019 I was in Kolkata, India for making some videos. Unfortunately, one of the meals I ate at a restaurant did not suit me and gave me a bacterial infection. As I travelled back home a few days later, I was very dehydrated and had to be hospitalized. More than the bacteria for which the prescribed antibiotics were working, the doctors at the hospital were worried about the depletion of sodium and potassium, and started me on an IV drip of sodium and injection of potassium. For a couple of days, while the IV drip lasted, I had copious hallucinations that I had previously experienced years ago only under a hallucinogenic drug.

My scientific curiosity was aroused and I made a quick hypothesis. Like hallucinogens, the IV drip of sodium to quickly make up for sodium deficiency puts the brain in a helter-skelter transition mode and the brain puts up a lot of noise like ink blots in a Rorschach. Confession: I never asked a doctor if this is true. The important thing is that there were hallucinations. How do they originate? Mind puts meaning in all that brain noise and consciousness tries to make sensible pictures that parade before us in our mind's sky; this is the experience that we call hallucination.

Hallucinations don't have to be meaningful; but here is the thing. I discovered as I played with them then: my intention could put order in them and kind of create the scenario that was at least partly my creation. Not an original creation, mind you, but creation based on an idea that I already had. I assume artists do the same kind of thing except they put form in the idea with paint and on a canvas.

And of course, we can do that, we do that, with dreams. Neuroscientists think dreams are what the brain makes out of the brain noise. I theorize, more correctly, that all dreams are created by consciousness using the mind to give meaning to the Rorschach of brain noise. In usual dreams, we do not actively participate in the dream story, but in lucid dreams we do.

Finally, schizophrenia. There is that neurochemical imbalance theory that psychiatrists love because that puts them in the driver's seat as far as treatment is concerned; nobody but a licensed doctor can prescribe drugs. In the seventies and eighties, humanistic and transpersonal psychologists however, had many attractive alternative psychological theories.

One such theory is the philosopher Gregory Bateson's double bind theory. Teen age girls under severe parental pressure, usually patriarchal, suffer oscillation of identity—good or bad—listen to what father wants or hear her own drum of who she wants to be. If the oscillations go wild, the girl can fall into a loop of madness.

What interested me in the eighties when I discovered the two modalities of the self—quantum self and the ego/persona—was the question: could the oscillation be between these two modes when we are in the middle of teen-age ego development?

After all these years, now I think that this alone is not enough. But suppose we put in some brain-in-transition and neurochemical imbalance that create hallucinations into the equation. With creative imagination, a teen-ager could easily manipulate the hallucinatory images to create an immensely liveable internal reality. When she succeeds, she is a genius. If she fails, she is living with hallucinations that she cannot control. Outer and inner—both have become nightmarish, and uncontrollable for her. She alternates between them but loses the ability of distinguishing between them. This is the onset of schizophrenia.

A thorough discussion of schizophrenia is beyond the scope of this book, but in the following two sections, I will elaborate more on all three experiences starting with drugs and ending with dreams.

II
Can Drugs Help with Consciousness Raising?

In 1981-82, Ron Graves, my ex graduate student, was instrumental in finding me a sabbatical job at AMAF industries in Columbia, MD. Ron also helped me to get settled there. And his wife Donnis was a darling. In private, my wife Maggie called them Ronnis and Donnis. What a crazy pair! Many of our evenings in Columbia we spent with them.

Ron and Donnis were the regular fixtures of our life. We played cards, the four of us. Sometimes, Ron would bring some good dope, marijuana called sansa mia or something like that, and we smoked.

My audiences today often ask me, did you achieve any wisdom from drugs? Did you do drugs at all? Do you do drugs now? I mention Ron because he initiated me to marijuana, *ganja*. In India, *ganja* is a part of the life of many spiritual hippies or hobos who are called *sadhus*. Technically, they are all renunciates, all spiritual practitioners, but in reality, it is a multicultural situation. I'd say the dominant *sadhu* culture is not really centred around spirituality; it is centred around drugs, especially marijuana.

With Ron's initiative, I have done marijuana many times; most times with Maggie, sometimes without her. And my experience is that not much happens with that particular drug. It is mostly a recreational drug. You relax, you feel no pain. But you see colours; that's a hallucinatory image. How I tried to manipulate it to make a meaningful experience!

Only one time did I make a breakthrough; I saw aura around people. Was it my creation of what I thought an aura should be like, or was it the visual perception of our bioelectric body that is now a well-established phenomenon? I do not know.

What did marijuana do to me that I could see aura? This is a scientific question and the answer should be obvious. The drug interacts with the brain; all drugs do that; and they alter the brain. The brain is our conduit to experience whatever potentiality there is to experience. It makes sense to try to alter the brain to see if changing the brain opens our doors of perception, enables us to collapse *different* potentialities than we do with our regular brain.

I gave up marijuana after it became clear that although it undoubtedly alters the brain and so opens us to new experiences, it also affects our judgment. Ron was visiting us in Eugene and as was his style, he got hold of some very potent dope, which Maggie promptly used to make some cookies. We each took one, but even after half an hour, no effect. Ron started doubting if the stuff was potent after all; so we all ate another cookie. Still no effect. We had a reservation for the local Hilton Hotel restaurant and being late was not an option on a Saturday night. We might lose the reservation. To make certain that we get at least a little buzz from the marijuana, we each took another cookie and took off.

We ordered food. Busy night at the restaurant, and the food was taking its time to arrive; so, Maggie went to the ladies' room. Just as she left, the food came. I took one bite, and suddenly, the marijuana hit. Wow! What a play of colours! I was thoroughly enjoying the sensations but something was nagging at me. Where was Maggie? It was not her style to spend so long in the bathroom. So, I got up looking for her. I did not have to go far.

Somebody was lying on the floor, a woman, and a crowd had formed around her. A waiter was asking if anyone knew her. Upon a hunch, I looked closely and of course it was my darling wife. But I was cautious. Marijuana was illegal. "I know her," I said. "She is a neighbour." Then I knelt down by Maggie and whispered, "What happened?" "I was coming back to the table and suddenly my knees gave way and here I am. I guess you know what did it."

Meanwhile, the waiter was asking me if he should call a doctor. To which I said nonchalantly, "No need. She says she did not eat any lunch. That must have made her weak." I was holding my breath, but the waiter bought my reasoning. He agreed that I should take her home but insisted on getting a wheelchair. As he was getting the wheelchair, I was looking for Ron. And he was found to be nowhere.

The wheelchair came and I took Maggie downstairs without any mishap, much relieved. Ron was waiting. Before I said anything, he said, "Hold it. More is not merrier in this case. Suppose they detected marijuana smell on me! It is a miracle that they didn't on you." Ok. I went to get the car with Ron watching Maggie's wheelchair.

I found the car but it was quite another thing to find my exit out of the underground garage. After circling back and forth for about ten times I finally figured out that the exit was on a floor down.

On the way back, I found that I could not gauge either time or distance any more, not at the level one needs for driving anyway. I was so scared to hit the car in front that I slowed down to snail speed. Fortunately, neither of my passengers could care less. That was it for me and marijuana.

I have never done LSD, but LSD is legendary as consciousness altering. LSD has opened so many Western scientific materialist minds to spirituality; my two heroes in the seventies, John Lilly and Ram Dass (ne Richard Alpert), both were virtually LSD addicts. John once told me that he seriously considered using LSD continuously to make temporary spiritual Oneness a permanent fixture of his life. Fortunately, he never actually put that idea to practice as far as I know.

Good thing too. My insight gained during my hospital experience under sodium IV drip is this: drugs are good to get a glimpse of the oneness the way you see it which is likely based on the opinion of many religious/spiritual teachers that you revere. But that's about it; you are recreating other people's experience into spiritual form by manipulating the otherwise hallucinatory images that people see under drugs. I don't deny the power of it! If it releases the grip of physicalism on you, great! If it enhances your creativity, even better. But don't think it is the authentic experience of the spiritual oneness that a quantum leap to the real quantum self-experience takes you.

I know. In the eighties, under the direction of a physician-friend, I did the drug ketamine a couple of times. And indeed, my intentions of penetrating the ego gave me an image of me going through the image of a big eye.

Unquestionably also, drugs cause physical or psychological dependence or both, and that can be disastrous to our physical and mental well-being. So, unless your attachment to physicality is very strong, it is better not to go the drug route.

III
Is Schizophrenia a Failure to act Creatively?

Gregory Bateson's double bind theory is another take on Plato's idea of a fundamental human problem: being human is to be in charge of two horses—one tamed, conditioned and predictable, the ego; the other creative and unpredictable, even wild, the quantum self. It is tempting to theorize that schizophrenia is the result of runaway oscillation between the creative and conditioned tendencies producing instability. Read the psychologist Paris Williams' immensely readable book to that effect, *Rethinking Madness*.

I intuit there is more to it than that. I have mentioned brain neurochemical imbalance which gives a few people a permanent brain in transition, with plenty of brain Rorschach to play with. If the creative aspect of the person is unbalanced, that is, if the conditioned repertoire that gives form to creative ideas are not as well developed as the aspect of production of ideas, then unbridled imagination willcreate hallucinogenic images with the Rorschach that have no bearing on reality.

If in addition, suppose the inner-outer integration, even the semblance of a balance between the two is also lacking. Suppose in addition, an authority figure, as in Bateson's double bind theory, has made the outer particularly unattractive, and uncontrollable, what happens then? Such a person will live more and more in the internal world of hallucinatory images of a made-up reality and soon lose the ability of distinguishing between them. This is schizophrenia.

The brain does not distinguish between imagination and actuality. So, if a schizophrenic's consciousness uses the mind to create hallucinogenic scary images, the brain will be triggered to play the instinctual fear and other negative emotional circuits and elicit the same negative response like violence as if the internal image was real.

In this way, schizophrenia results from a failed attempt to penetrate the first layer of reality and live in a self-created internal world. Schizophrenics penetrate the outer and identify with an "unreal" inner that they cannot discern from the real.

IV
Dreams: Integrating the Inner and the Outer

Dreams are another story; they are built into our regular life as regular experiences during periods of sleep whose signature is rapid eye movement, REM sleep.

Dreams are mental experiences. To be sure consciousness uses brain noise to make visual images, but it is our mind that gives meaning to these images. Therefore, dreams are all about your meaning life—how your mind is giving meaning to both your external and your internal experiences in an ongoing manner. So, it behoves you to pay attention to dreams. A very consorted way to integrate your outer and inner life is to pay attention to dreams.

Penetrating the physical layer of reality is not about leaving it for a better one that you create. You have to integrate the inner and the outer and make both better places to live.

Dream Psychology

Please comprehend what I said already: we make our dream pictures from the Rorschach of white noise that the electromagnetic activities of the brain provide. What we see in a dream is what meaning mind gives to this white noise.

According to Jung, dreams tell us about the great myths that run through our lives. Many others believe that dreams help formulate and perpetuate personal myths that we create and that we live by.

An example of such a myth is the Hero's Journey. The hero rejects his or her environmental and cultural conditioning and leaves to find his or her own meaning. The hero achieves his or her goal after a lot of effort; finally, the hero returns.

Who dreams? Consciousness dreams by converting waves of possibility into the actual events of the dreams and in the process of conversion dividing itself into two parts: one part, the dreamer sees itself separate from the objects of its experience, the other part, dream objects.

Dreams jump around from episode to episode without any apparent causal continuity whatsoever. In contrast to the apparent fixity of waking awareness where quantum uncertainty is camouflaged, dreams retain their quantum nature to a much larger extent, only yielding somewhat to Newtonian fixity because of ego conditioning. In dreams, we do have some conditioned continuity and this gives us the story line of a particular dream episode. But when the episode changes, we have the opportunity to experience the causal discontinuity of quantum actualization. In truth, however, very often there is a subtle continuity even in episodic change.

This brings us to another question that philosophers ask: when we wake up from a dream, we return to the same waking reality (with minor changes), but when we go back to dreaming, seldom do we encounter the same dream reality; so how can dream reality be taken seriously? The answer to this question is that dreams speak to us about the mind--their concerns are meaning, meaning of the physical, the vital, the mental, the supramental, and even the quantum self and ultimately oneness--consciousness itself. So, we have to look for continuity not in content, but in meaning. When we do that, we can readily see that most often, especially during the same night, we do return to the same dream reality in terms of meaning. The contents and images change, but the associated meanings retain continuity.

In this way psychotherapists who encourage their clients to engage in dream work mainly at the meaning level are doing something right. The implicit assumption that these psychotherapists working with their clients' dreams make is that all meaning that emerges upon analysis of the dream symbols is the most significant when it resonates with the dreamer. The gestalt psychologist Fritz Perls summarizes this attitude best when he says, "All the different parts of the dream are yourself, a projection of yourself." Quantum science agrees; a dream symbol is a projection of yourself to the extent that it represents only the personal meaning that you attribute to that symbol in the overall context of the dream with proper attention given to the feeling and archetypal aspects. Especially important are the other human characters in your dream. When you see your wife in a dream, she is you, that part of you which is like your perception of your wife. Of course, there are also universal contextual symbols (usually the Jungian archetypes of the collective unconscious) representing the universal themes that appear in people's dreams in which case we universally project the same meaning. The themes of archetypal dreams are codified in our mythologies, such themes as the hero's journey.

The meaning level of our life is playing also in our waking events, but we get so side-tracked by the clamour of the fixed meaning of our symbols in waking life, that we seldom pay attention to their deep meanings. For example, suppose one day you have an out-of-the-ordinary number of encounters with stop signs while driving; would you stop to think that this may be some kind of synchronicity! Dreams give you a second chance. The same night you may dream that you are driving your car and then you come across a stop sign! Upon waking up, you may easily realize that the car is representing your ego and the stop sign is attracting your attention to put a stop to your rampant egotism.

Dreams give us an Ongoing Report about the health of our five bodies in the five layers of reality

Most dreams can be much better analysed and understood if dealt with from the quantum science viewpoint of the five bodies of ourselves, one body in each layer of reality--the physical, the (vital) energy body, the mental body, the supramental themes that we embody in our soul software – the higher vital – higher mental body , and the bliss body of quantum self, leading to oneness.

1. Physical body dreams: These are the so-called day residue dreams whose dominant concern is the

physical body and the physical world, those memories of the waking events which did not arrive at closure.

2. Vital body dreams: nightmares in which the dominant quality is a strong emotion such as fear. The analysis of vital body dreams can teach us about our suppressed traumas.

3. Mental body dreams: dreams in which the meaning of the symbols, rather than the content dominates. Good examples are pregnancy dreams and flying dreams. Many recurring dreams (not counting nightmares) fall into this category also. These dreams tell us about the meaning of our "meaning life", the ongoing saga of our mind, and mental blocks.

4. Supramental theme dreams: dreams that contain objective universal symbols, the Jungian archetypes for example. These dreams tell us about the ongoing exploration and unfolding of the meaning of archetypal themes of our lives. Reincarnation theory shows (read my book *Physics of the Soul*) that some of us bring an intention to engage with a chosen archetype when we take birth; this is called our *dharma*, spelled with small d. If you don't know what your dharma—the archetype of your current life—is, pay attention to these dreams.

5. Bliss body dreams--These are rare dreams in which the dreamer wakes up with a deep sense of bliss, grounded in Being.

Integrating Inner and Outer with the help of dreams

In the eighties, I went through an intense period of cleansing my internal ecosystem. I saw all kinds of purgative dreams in that period; working with a teacher on those dreams really helped me. I still remember the last dream I saw in that series.

In the dream, two characters appeared. One was Ronald Reagan, a very conservative American politician, and the other was the actress Jane Fonda, a very liberal person. But what stood out in the dream, is not who the characters were. Well here was a president, and here was a famous actress, but all they were doing was dancing around detritus. Literally. The ground they were walking on was full of excrement. I woke up with the feeling that okay, being liberal or being conservative is all shit. It is following somebody else's opinion. And I was ready to give up somebody else's opinion influencing who I was. My slate was thus clean, so I could get into discovering my own opinion through real creativity—fundamental creativity. After this episode ended, I seldom saw another excrement dream.

Not too long after all this cleansing took place, I went through a phase of flying dreams, creativity became important to me in those days. Then there was a phase of "naked" dreams; I would be naked in public and had to deal with my embarrassment. I went through a lot of authenticity training in that phase. I am convinced this improved my creativity. From then on, dreams and synchronicity have always been a dynamic duo of helpers to me in my creative journey.

I had a supramental "body" dream that bears on my future. In my dream, I was there, but the overwhelming presence was that of a radiant man, so radiant that I could not help but look at him, and look, and look, feeling bliss the whole time. Even upon waking, the bliss and joy persisted. When I told the dream to my dream teacher, he looked at me kind of funny with his eyes growing big, "Amit, don't you get it? You were looking at your own enlightened self," he said with not a little awe in his voice.

This radiant energy body is not only in my future but in everybody's future!

Dreams and your personal archetype—dharma

I hope you remember the concept of dharma introduced above. In my workshops, I always teach people some basic dream analysis with the motivation of uncovering the archetype of their choice from the previous incarnation. First, I give them the task of making the intention that they want to find their personal archetype in a dream before going to sleep. I also tell them to keep a notebook with a penlight to write the dream down, at least one line, upon waking from the dream. Next day, they share their dreams with me, together we do a little analysis until it clicks with the dreamer, and voila, they find their dharma/archetype more often than not.

The Experiences of Dreams, Drugs, and Schizophrenia

Under the hypnosis of scientific materialism, we at once have a drug culture of pharmaceutical medicine that heals only temporarily but leaves you forever burdened with suffering side effects and a culture that is fearful of a class of drugs that arouse hallucinations. The same hypnosis teaches us to ignore our dream life calling it pointless. And psychiatrists label schizophrenia as entirely due to brain neurochemical imbalances that can only be treated by drugs.

The Quantum worldview validates dreams as an ongoing description of the unfolding of meaning in our lives. It also tells us that hallucinations are dream-like experiences produced by a brain in transition. Just as one can learn partial conscious control over dreams in the form of lucid dreams and use dreams for creativity, so can one learn to control drug-generated hallucinations enough to reenact creative and spiritual ideas about who we are, visions that enable us to penetrate the various sheaths that obscure reality.

Schizophrenia in this worldview is more than neurochemical imbalance which does produce a brain in transition. Schizophrenics try to escape from the trauma and double-bind situations of the physical external reality (for example that caused by authoritative parenting in the form of childhood traumas) to a liveable internal world via creatively manipulating the hallucinations but fail and get trapped. With understanding, our ability to heal schizophrenia may not be very far off.

Chapter 7
Penetrating the Mental and Vital Layers

I
Penetrating sheaths: What does that Mean?

The Upanishads look at the five layers of reality as sheaths of ignorance. Penetrating a sheath in this language not only means having new experiences but also something more. At the same time, one has to integrate the previous layer or sheath into one's new way of living. Otherwise when you go back and forth between the layers, part of life you know, you won't be at ease. For today's people, the rational mind dominates us so much that many of us are not even aware of feelings in the body; as I confessed, I was one of those people. Today, many young people are information junkies; they are not in touch with either the mental meanings or the vital energies.

So, we teach people quantum worldview and they begin to wake up to their creative potential and reap the reward of exploring their potentialities. Meaning comes back in their lives, as does purpose. Along with meaning and purpose comes a new source of happiness—satisfaction.

Simultaneously, we become aware of the peculiar situation in the brain-based life. Our meaning processing has a conscious component. On the other hand, we process emotions at the mid-brain, and quite unconsciously. Most of the emotions are negative. However, we do experience positive emotions in the form of pleasure. Both these experiences are built in the mid-brain; they are conditioned and are often aroused unconsciously in us.

When can we say we have penetrated the vital or the mental sheath? Only when we have achieved a dynamic balance between creativity and conditioning in these domains of experience. For the second sheath, this means experiencing feelings in the body at the navel, and the heart chakras, and exploring creativity at these chakras as well. For the third sheath, it involves exploring new meaning in known archetypal contexts. When we explore the archetypes of goodness and love initially using known contexts, and make representations of the insights with both new feelings and new meanings, this enables us to build positive emotional brain circuits that can balance negative emotions. When that happens, paying proper attention to rationality without suppressing emotions becomes possible. But that still keeps us in the lower layers of the vital and the mental.

Something else can happen too at this stage. We can explore rationality with positive emotion—passion. When we add passion to rational curiosity, it opens the door to fundamental creativity for the exploration of archetypes. We have begun the journey to enter the fourth layer—the world of archetypal experiences, intuitions and insights.

II
The Quantum Principles of Transformation

So far so good. But when you come to exploring the inner experiences with your brain and the body expecting quantum behaviour, at first you will be disappointed. Except for internality, your vital experiences of feeling and mental experiences of meaning have a lot in common with physical experiences. They, too, are often quite predictable, if not in detail, but in essence.

Why is that? Because there is conditioning due to processing of the experiences in the mirror of past memory before we experience them in our ego. The I of the quantum self becomes I/me of the ego as a result of the preconscious processing (see chapter 9 for details). The "me" has learned traits—our character and habit patterns. The I/me is local; it robs us not only of the nonlocality of the quantum self but also of the tangled hierarchy replacing it with a simple hierarchy. What presides over the simple hierarchy of programs is our ego/character/persona. Moreover, when thoughts come from past memory, they appear more or less continuous; discontinuity vanishes from our internal experience.

So just exploring the internal is not enough. If all those quantum signatures are gone, your materialistic doubts will return: could thoughts and feelings be Newtonian after all, could they be brain and body phenomena after all? Do we really need to invent quantum nonphysical mental and vital potentiality for understanding them?

There is another way to put the materialist concern: we have software associated with the body organs; epigenetic they may be, they still are physical; we have them and our organs function satisfactorily because of them, thank you. And the same can be said about the brain: we have the mental software and it could very well be a brain product. By creating permutations and combinations of them, we can create a lot of new possibilities that can explain our capacity for imagination and even some creativity. So again, we wonder: Do we really need to postulate a nonphysical mind?

Still another way to put it is this: We are happy with the base-level human condition as is: me centeredness, negative emotions, pleasure and information addiction. We can and will use technology to make it better. Who needs those so hard to practice "spiritual" stuff like meditation? After centuries of battling against religion, we finally are able to indulge in permissive societies. Who needs moderation back in our lives even though in the form of scientific spirituality?

See how persistent materialism is? How do we bring the empowering elements of the quantum worldview to bear on our internal experiences? Before answering, let me indulge in a little diversion, another story from the Upanishads.

The story of *Manava, Danava*, and the *Deva*

This story from the Upanishads of India is very telling about how we can make changes, but I have to make some introductory comments first:

In India, the hierarchical me-centred apathetic ego-persona that uses the *guna* of *tamas (conditioning)* is called the human-person—*manava*. Overuse of *tamas*, too much use of sociocultural conditioning and lack of creativity in processing meaning has a dumbing down effect.

The aspect of the human being that uses this quality of processing meaning with situational creativity or rajas is called *danava* in Sanskrit. The *danava's* problem is hyperactivity—fickleness. The danavas get attached to their negative emotions and are often cruel, violent, and dominating. Additionally, often they learn to use their pleasure circuits in conjunction with their negative emotional circuits. In other words, they derive pleasure from other people's discomfort, the ultimate use of domination.

Indians call the fundamentally creative *sattva guna* of the human being *deva*. But the excessive misuse of it develops intellectualism—a detachment from the body. Ideally, the *deva*-dominated people should look for the intuitive part of human experiences, but the problem is to get stuck in the mind's rational intellect. Too much analysis. *Devas* also lack awareness of feelings in the body. That makes them vulnerable to emotions the way the brain processes them— pleasure and negative emotions. *Devas* suppress the latter and indulge in the former.

Here is the story. All three, *manava, danava,* and *deva* see a strange being sitting on a hilltop, a being with considerable power emanating from it. Naturally "what's in it for me" speaks up in each of the aspects of the human being in the form of the question, "How can I overcome the deficiency I have developed through the excessive misuse of my given quality and get back my power?"

First the *tamasic* aspect of the human person asks, "How can I access my power?" The being says, "*Da.*" It is an intuition you see, subject to interpretation by the mind. The *manava* understands the intuition this way. Da stands for the Sanskrit *datta* meaning give. The human-person is constricted by the me-centeredness and apathy. Giving expands consciousness.

Now the *danava* approaches the being and asks the same question. The being answers, "*Da.*" To danava, Da stands for the Sanskrit word *dayaddhama* meaning have mercy. Cultivate positive emotions like compassion to balance some of those negative emotions. The balance even in part will restore the ability for situational creativity and transformation.

Finally, the turn of the *deva*. Same, question, same answer, "*Da.*" For *deva*, "*Da*" stands for the Sanskrit word *damayata* meaning restrain. Restrain yourself from too much rationalization and too much molecular pleasure. Then room will be made for subtler forms of happiness that requires the creative exploration of the archetypes.

If this sounds like a progressive initiation into progressive transformation, it is.

They are good recipes to be sure. But they are not compelling, nor do they do the job adequately. Can we do any better with quantum science?

Fortunately, my research and exploration of quantum science and consciousness for four decades tell me yes. We can.

So, what does quantum science say to the *manava*?

Today's *manava* has an additional problem: too much information processing, even further dumbing down. Too much use of machine intelligence and too little of human contact. So not only does the *manava* have to expand his consciousness but also has to shift his interest from information to meaning. Develop some mental intelligence and also, renew acquaintance with feeling.

Giving is excellent recipe for expanding your consciousness and in quantum lingo it takes you to discover in yourself an aspect that you thought you lost since childhood: nonlocality. Nonlocality, remember, is signalless communication. Why is that important for transformation? Communication in space and time require signals which, by scientific law, move at a finite speed, taking at least a little time. In contrast, signalless communication is instantaneous. Behold! Instant communication means communicating with your own self. Giving and nonlocality expands our consciousness to include the other as if the other is you. They help us to see unity with others.

The quantum worldview says this: we human beings have the potentiality of being one with everybody else using this nonlocal communication. Naturally cultivating nonlocality will help to expand your me-centredness. In trying to cultivate nonlocality you will discover that centring on communication with meaning and understanding also helps.

You will also discover the feeling dimension of yourself, where nonlocality comes easily.

In the brain your me-centeredness expresses itself as activities in the brain areas that neuroscientists identify as belonging to the self-agency. The reinforced memories of ego-persona that feed your "me" are stored in these areas. In the body your self-centeredness expresses yourself as vitality tied up to the navel chakra—the welfare of you and you alone. Narcissism. For women, vitality is tied up in the heart chakra producing too much neediness, needing another to attach to.

Giving, giving unconditionally, obviously takes you away from the thoughts of the me-personas. It also balances the energy between your navel chakra and your heart chakra.

Giving is just one practice; another practice you can do is the practice of not taking yourself so seriously—humility. Still another one is forgiveness. All these practices also help one to gain self-respect instead of self-indulgence.

Look at the scale of happiness that the psychologist Sunita Pattani and I have constructed (fig. 19). Level 0 and 1 are about mentally ill people, and level 2 is normal. Unfortunately, the base level human condition with all that negativity preference built into the brain will always tend to go toward 2^-. Bringing nonlocality in life lifts one to 2^+.

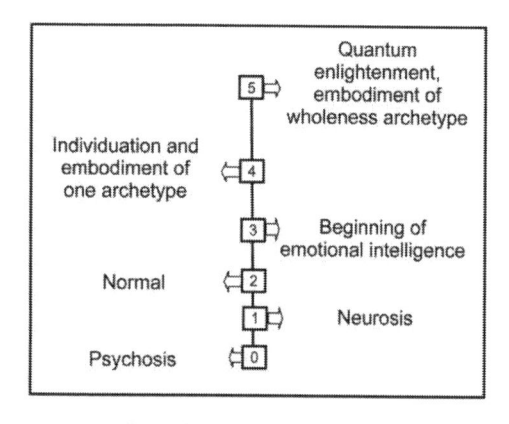

```
                    Quantum
                    enlightenment,
              ┌─┐   embodiment of
              │5│⇨  wholeness archetype
              └─┘
Individuation and │
embodiment of ⇦┌─┐
one archetype  │4│
               └─┘
                │
              ┌─┐
              │3│⇨ Beginning of
              └─┘  emotional intelligence
               │
    Normal  ⇦┌─┐
             │2│
             └─┘
               │
              ┌─┐
              │1│⇨ Neurosis
              └─┘
               │
 Psychosis  ⇦┌─┐
             │0│
             └─┘
```

fig. 19: The scale of happiness

And then one can give up information processing to avoid boredom and concentrate on meaning. This begins with understanding—bringing your own meaning giving capacity of the mind to play. Once this becomes fun, one can develop an interest in the archetypes.

Transforming the *Danava*

Next, let's address the *danava* in us. In the quantum worldview, movement can be continuous which is familiar to you, right? Thoughts and feelings all move continuously in your experience. But a discontinuous quantum leap is allowed in the quantum worldview. It is via these quantum leaps of thoughts and feelings that you learn to make positive emotional brain circuits to balance negativity.

The *danava* in us has the ability to engage in what we call situational creativity. This is creativity within a fixed archetypal context given by somebody else—a teacher, a good book, a workshop, what have you. It is about finding a new meaning and new feeling associated with the archetype, within that given archetypal context, a new feeling and new meaning that you manifest in your living.

Say you are exploring compassion within the context that Jesus gives: love your neighbour. Your neighbour is a lonely old man, and you invite him to dinner. Old stuff will come up: what's in it for me? Will this fellow reciprocate the dinner? Suppose he expects to be invited back? It is this old pattern of thinking, your old patterns that you are trying to replace with a more compassionate character. So, proceed. Work on opening your heart and search for new meanings for what comes up.

To open your heart even to this extent you have to discover feelings in the body and their body centres—the chakras. You have to discover that if you are not so miserly, so anal retentive, the energy from your low first two chakras do not have to collapse at the navel. Instead, they can go all the way up to the heart and collapse. That's when you get the feeling of compassion—to be passionate with somebody else.

The creative process is do-be-do-be-do. Do is what I described in the previous paragraph. But "being" is hard for the *danava* in us—the problem is hyperactivity. The tendency is to do-do-do. To make room for "be" you engage with concentration meditation, focusing on an object. Initially, your thoughts quickly follow one another (fig. 20a). Meditating regularly for a while slows you down (fig. 20 b); between thoughts you will now have gaps.

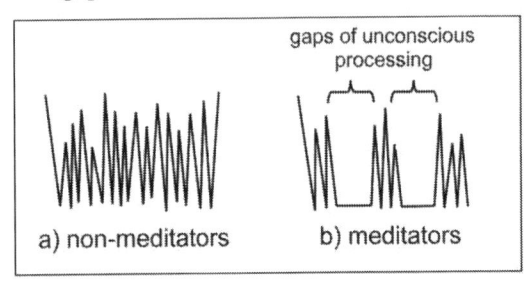

fig. 20: How meditation slows down thoughts: (a) frequency of thoughts for a non-meditator; (b) the frequency of thoughts for a meditator

Can one build positive emotional brain circuits this creative way, balance the negative and transform? You bet. There is now brain evidence of this shift in the scale of happiness: in happier people activity shifts from the unconscious right brain to the conscious left brain. This transformed station of life is happiness level 3.

The Transforming Task of the *Deva* is harder

Now let's talk about the deva's transformation. Restraining from pleasure opens us to other alternative ways to happiness—feeling, meaning, and archetypes. Engaging fundamental creativity to explore the archetypes eventually leads to the intuitive mind, a mind whose primary mode of cognition is intuition. Intuition engages the quantum self in us—living in tangled hierarchy.

When you relate to another with pleasure seeking in mind, you objectify your other. You are the head honcho of the relationship; the other's job is to please you. To make a tangled hierarchy that is a circular relationship, you need to discover the otherness of the other and respect that otherness. Restraining pleasure is a big first step to all this transformation coming your way.

There is also another problem. The creative mode of the *deva* in us is fundamental creativity. And the creative process is the same do-be-do-be-do. In the be-phase, we relax in the waking state to give unconscious processing a chance. During relaxation, the brain's tendency, and fMRI studies prove this, is to go back to the command of what they call self-agency and what we call the ego-character-persona. So, the old ego-habits such as engagement with rational intellectualism to avoid boredom comes back. Also, all that suppression-repression emotional stuff comes back too. It is these tendencies that the deva has to avoid; deva has to clean up the personal unconscious, engage in what Jung called shadow cleansing. In archetypal terms, this is when we invite the Hindu archetype of goddess Kali symbolic of the cleaning up of the dark light-shutting part of the personal unconscious in our life.

The brain, neuroscientists find, is very predictable. You have a task, it will be in the attention mode; you relax, the brain returns to the occupation with the ego-character-persona.

The quantum solution is again: tangled hierarchy. We turn to the quantum tangled hierarchical self. How? Through watching our boredom, our intellect and pleasure-seeking mind, but passively without interfering. This awareness training or witnessing meditation takes us away from the self-agency toward the quantum self.

Once we are open to the quantum self this way, once our ego has become authentic free of all the inauthentic personalities that separate, the ego is ready to play with the quantum self to embody the insights gained as quantum leaps of fundamental creativity. In other words, to live in flow—a state of alternative inspiration and perspiration without any seam.

It happens. There is now brain evidence of people living in flow; these people's increased alertness shows up in a jump of brain wave frequency from beta (14-30 Hz) to gamma of over 40 Hz. I put such people who live in flow in happiness levels of 4 and 5.

In summary, we establish nonlocality for the manava in our lives mainly through the practice of meditation with others; we need community for that. To transform the danava in us, we take discontinuous quantum leaps via creativity with a teacher, call her a guru if you like. Then as deva, we explore tangled hierarchy via relationship with others and eventually via flow-relationship between the two poles of our own self (fig. 21).

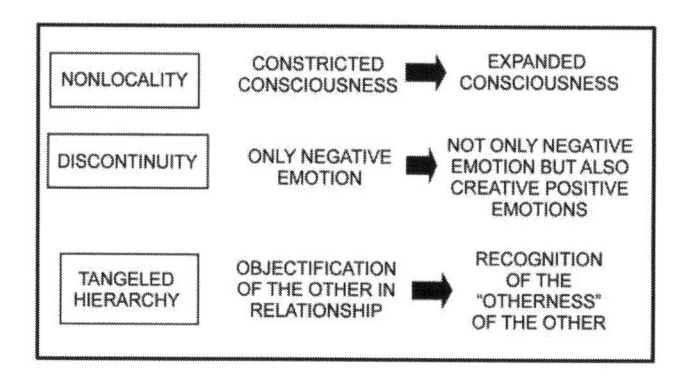

NONLOCALITY	CONSTRICTED CONSCIOUSNESS ➡	EXPANDED CONSCIOUSNESS
DISCONTINUITY	ONLY NEGATIVE EMOTION ➡	NOT ONLY NEGATIVE EMOTION BUT ALSO CREATIVE POSITIVE EMOTIONS
TANGELED HIERARCHY	OBJECTIFICATION OF THE OTHER IN RELATIONSHIP ➡	RECOGNITION OF THE "OTHERNESS" OF THE OTHER

fig. 21: How the three quantum principles of human transformation are used to change the three aspects of the human condition

Chapter 8
Discovering the Fourth Layer: The World of the Archetypes

I
Intuitions and Archetypes

Our intuitions come from a special domain of transcendent potentiality—the supra-mental land of the archetypes—to which we dive from our mind to mine the hidden treasures of the quantum unconscious—the forever new archetypal potentialities. As we plunge into that unknown world, taking a quantum leap from the ordinary mind, we encounter precious jewels of formless entities. These are the archetypal themes of value—the contexts of meaning and feeling that form the essence of creative work. As we bring them back through creative insights, and manifest forms to take shape around the formless archetypes—bells ring, joy reverberates, and a creative act of discovery is completed.

Our evolution so far has produced the brain which can map the mind, but alas! We have no way to make direct physical representations of the supramental archetypes. Mental (and vital energy) maps of them are the best we can do. Since there is no direct memory of our archetypal experiences, these experiences never get conditioned via any reflection in the mirror of memory. In this way, the quantum self is always associated with supramental experiences of intuitions and insights.

Behold! The quantum self is not a stranger to us; every time we have an intuition, which is a supra-mental experience, it is a beckoning of the quantum self. So as creatives, we learn to value our intuitions, our window to the archetypal "soul" values. We then manifest the soul values with situational and fundamental creativity ending up with positive emotional brain circuits—part of soul-making.

One of the strange changes in the societal atmosphere is that today only religious people talk about religious or spiritual values that are pretty much the same thing as archetypes. Why don't all people talk about archetypes and values? This is one of the places where scientific materialism has caused a huge distortion in people's mind everywhere. Imagine this! A few scientists, sitting mainly in the academes of USA Eastern seaboard have done what the British imperialists could not do. A new ubiquitous valueless Intellectual Imperialism? You bet.

Today academics everywhere are sold on scientific materialism which undermines the archetypes except to say something lame like values come from our evolutionary history by some kind of a play of our survival motif. But of course, if the archetypal values originated in this way, they could not be timeless, could they? So, sociologists of the materialist ilk try to find dubious evidence of how our archetypal values have changed over the various eras of human civilization. No, the archetypes have not changed; their mental representations have gotten better (and worse, as in the hands of scientific materialists).

It seems that most people today no longer look at truth as timeless and absolute with disastrous consequences to society. If truth were not absolute, how would physical laws remain the same over all times? The quantum worldview asserts the absolute nature of truth that gives truth-value to all archetypes of the supramental land. The quantum worldview also holds that embodying the archetypes even in the form of representations made by the vital and mental—soul-making--is the next great evolutionary step that human beings need to take.

The author Mark Harrison wrote a book, *The American Evolution*, where he talked about the right to choose a lawful calling. If you hear the calling of an archetype in an intuitive experience, you should be able to follow through in a lawful way (without harming anyone else). You should be given opportunities to follow through.

This is one of those taken for granted rights not enumerated in any Constitution or Bill of Rights, like the right to privacy. We may need quantum activism in every country to enable such a right. We need to exercise it if we are to make social change and bring our social systems in synch with the movement of consciousness.

There is an impending need to replace transactional education by transformational education at all levels, but the regulations make it very difficult even for higher education. We need to exercise this right to choose our archetypal calling and let it be tested by the courts, which will see reason much faster as it did in the case of abortion and the right to privacy in America.

II
The Nine Major Archetypes

Archetypes are the highest contexts of thinking and feeling. What is a context? To get the idea consider the word "ass" in the following two sentences:

The ass is a useful domestic animal

Get off your ass

The meaning of the word *ass* changes drastically depending on the context we use it in a sentence, doesn't it?

Einstein gave another wonderful example of context. If you are listening to a lecture that you consider boring, time seems to become so slow, "always going and never gone." If you are with your sweetheart, on the other hand, time seems to pass so quickly.

Abraham Maslow gave us the concept of hierarchy of needs. Our lower needs, he said, are survival needs. If we are into the survival mode, we miss the point of the archetypes. For example, in the survival mode, we may look at the archetype of abundance in material terms—The American dream—a good house, a good job etc. In this mode, the archetype of love becomes sexuality. But when our survival need is satisfied, we realize material abundance is never enough to make us feel you have abundance. We need to satisfy higher needs to get a feeling of having abundance. In this way, the archetypes open us to higher contexts of living. What was a search for possession of an archetypal value, becomes its exploration.

Sexual love is about possessing love objects, conquesting sexual partners as objects of "my" pleasure. When me/my consciousness expands to include the other, sexuality gives way to a mutual exploration of love.

There are nine important archetypes for us to explore and embody: abundance, power, goodness, love, justice, Truth, beauty, wholeness, and self. I have spelled Truth with a capital T because it turns out that Truth is absolute, non-changing. Since the other archetypes share the same archetypal land with Truth, archetypes, in general, have truth-value in all of their many faces.

These nine archetypes by and large define the professions human being engage with to this day: business people explore abundance, politicians explore the archetype of power, people of clergy explore goodness, lawyers and judges explore justice, scientists, philosophers, and news media people explore Truth, artists, writers, and musicians explore beauty, everyone explores love, healers and teachers explore wholeness, spiritualseekers explore the self.

I left out a couple of professions, for example actors and engineers. They are Jacks of all trades, explorers of all the archetypes. Some of the archetypes open up with new possibilities only when they are explored with another archetype. For example, when abundance, power, and justice are explored with love!

Some of the archetypes have been subject to a splitting in dualities by our ancestors that became stabilized in our collective unconscious; the good-evil split is such a major split, and there has been much racism connected with beauty/ugly split. More recently, the absolute nature of the Truth archetype has been challenged giving us the true-false duality. This one is not universal yet and one hopes it never gets to be that way.

Now let's consider each of the major archetypes individually. I have written about them in earlier books. What I present below is drawn heavily from these earlier expositions.

III
The Quantum Nature of Archetypes

Intuitions are such fleeting experiences that it is hard to subject them to scientific study. Even so their quantum nature is obviously demonstrated by these two facts: 1) they are internal experiences; and 2) their nonlocality is demonstrable; it is not entirely unusual for two people to get the same intuition, for example, identical twins often report such things. And scientists are well known to discover the same laws in slightly different garb; the discovery of quantum physics by Werner Heisenberg and Erwin Schrodinger in slightly different representations is a good example of that.

The easiest way to convince yourself that archetypes are quantum objects is to explore them via the creative process yourself and see that it is always a discontinuous movement—call it a quantum leap—that leads you to its discovery in its original nature (fundamental creativity).

Suddenness, characterized by aha surprise is no doubt a spectacular aspect of creativity—both fundamental and situational, and led to the myth that only geniuses can engage in creativity. But make no mistake about it: creativity comes as a result of a process. As we now understand the process with the help of quantum physics, creativity, even fundamental creativity, has become accessible to everyone.

IV
The Archetype of Truth

One of our most important archetypal values is truth. Seek and ye shall find, and you will be troubled! Said Jesus. What bothers us about the message of an intuition is its truth-value. If we follow up our troubled minds and engage creativity, the products will express a transcendent truth—this truth is a common aspect of the archetypal themes. "My country is truth," intuited the poet Emily Dickinson who was no stranger to archetypes. Everybody, be aware!

Confusion arises because often what a poet or artist portrays does not look like what we ordinarily call truth. The face of the artist's truth is, as the Russian painter Wassily Kandinsky said, "constantly moving in slow motion." This is because the "whole" truth is transcendent, no perfect description of it is possible in manifest reality. Heed what the novelist Herman Hesse reminds us in these lines in his novel *Siddhartha*:

> Everything that is thought and expressed in words is one-sided, only half-truth; it all lacks totality, completeness, unity. When the illustrious Buddha taught about the world, he had to divide it into Samsara and *Nirvana*, into illusion and truth, into suffering and salvation. One cannot do otherwise; there is no other method for those who teach. But the world itself, being in and around us, is never one-sided. Never is a man or deed wholly Samsara or *Nirvana*. (p. 112)

Reality consists of both worlds of *Nirvana* and Samsara, both the transcendent (potentiality) and the immanent (manifestation); our creativity attempts to express the transcendent archetypes in the relativity of the immanent feelings and meanings. It never quite succeeds. A television character, trying to explain his garbled statement, said, "You should have heard it before I said it." Strangely, he had a point. Mental expression of an intuition compromises its truth-value.

Even our scientific laws do not express perfect archetypal truth, the whole truth. Science progresses when old laws yield to new ones as interpretations of the data change or better theory and new data emerge, ever extending the domains of science. You are witnessing one such worldview-change right now, in this book.

Realizing that one of the goals of creativity is to bring transcendent truth into embodiment—developing a product based on the creative insight is a must for a creative act. The product enables the creator to share the discovered truth with others; this sharing is part and parcel of creative purposiveness. This is true of the inner creativity of transformation as well. Gandhi said, "My life is my message." This is the spirit of inner transformation.

Today, what we have instead is the distortion of the timeless value of truth in science and media. If science itself says that truth is relative, then naturally the value of truth is undermined, and we get the American Fox News. We create false news and then we accuse others of false news in feigned surprise and outrage.

Here are the cartoonist Stephan Pastis' words describing the situation wonderfully in the comic strip *Pearls before Swine*. By the way the archetype of truth appears in the cartoon in an attire that can pass as that of a holy man; he is holding a lighted lantern:

Truth cries out, "Citizens, citizens, can I have a word with you?" Citizens gather around him; this part is easy even today. Truth continues, "I am Truth. I've taken a real beating lately."

A woman asks, "What happened?"

Says Truth, "Tweets, social media, television. People everywhere are lying more effectively than ever before."

Another citizen asks, "What do we do Mr. Truth?"

Truth replies, "Question things. Question sources. Pay for [real] journalism. Read history. Read critically. Because if you don't, things are gonna get much, much worse."

Everybody goes quiet for a bit. In the last frame, one of the regular characters of the comic strip Rat reports to another, Pig, "Then we yawned and beat him to death with his lantern." The pig says, "The Truth hurts." And the character Pigita concludes, "He was probably a socialist fascist terrorist."

With the idea of truth-value for our science and the importance of creativity to arrive at those values, we can fight back against the cynicism that pervades our society today. Having timeless truths to pursue once again will result in big dividends for societies everywhere: This is a quantum shield against undue societal influence exerted by elitists, lobbyists, and the media. Social leaders of a past era had moral authority: Where did that come from? Like the poet Emily Dickinson, they too lived in the land of truth.

Now of course, there is no denying that if your truth comes from other people's values, even lived values, not your own, your truth will always be relative truth. In this way, although traditionally we do not expect our leaders to be particularly creative, the times are changing. If you want your society to evolve to quantum society, if you want to have moral authority behind what you say, you'd better engage creativity. You better walk your talk. You better become a leader.

"Truth is that which touches the heart," said the novelist William Faulkner. In order to become a quantum leader of society, you should also heed what Faulkner is saying. The heart refers to the archetype of love—traditionally called a feminine value. But remember, the era of the intuitive mind is aborning with the demand that we learn to integrate the head and the heart. In Jungian psychological terms, this also involves integrating the male and the female within us.

V
The Archetypes of Abundance

The economist Adam Smith first proposed that the "invisible hands" of the free market, if left alone, would establish equilibrium between production and consumption, stabilize prices, and even allocate the resources among the different sectors of the economy. Leave the producers and consumers to follow the lead of their selfish interests; that and the invisible hands are all there is to capitalism.

What is this mysterious invisible hand of the free market? Materialists claim it must have its origin in material forces, but it is difficult to see how.

If truth were told, capitalism has failed twice in a big way since its inception and in many little ways in a more or less ongoing manner. I am of course talking about the Great Depression and the recent great recession and the many cycles of boom and bust. Why do the invisible hands stop acting periodically? No economist seems to know.

The free market has not been free since the great depression. We are encroaching on its freedom via government intervention. President Roosevelt started it by implementing demand-side economics. Increase demand by creating government-funded infrastructure jobs and unemployment insurance in recession time. Conservatives objected then, and decades later, unabashedly proposed their own supply-side intervention during Reagan's presidency: tax cuts for the rich. Do these interventions work? The supply-side intervention has yet to succeed even once. The demand-side intervention sometimes works, but sometimes doesn't.

If you look at economics from the vantage point of the quantum worldview, you immediately see the nature of the invisible hands—it is the purposive evolutionary movement of consciousness. The invisible hands don't work in a major way for the market economy if the participants are not acting in keeping with the purpose of conscious evolution, which if you remember is to make better and better representation of the archetypes. And that includes creativity and ethical behaviour. If you look at the causes of the Great Depression and the recent great recession, it checks out. Both of these events were caused by major shark-attack of greed and major lapses of ethics. They involved not creative products but artificial products of the rational mind such as stocks and derivatives of stocks.

So, economics has to be formulated from the get-go in a way that includes ethics and the social good, and also creativity; then the economy will be stable.

Business people engage in the economy for the selfish interest of making money—this is in accordance with Adam Smith's capitalism. Movement of consciousness demands that business people must explore an archetype. Money is the material representation of the archetype of abundance. Economics must serve the archetype of abundance, not only its material representation, money, but also its subtle representations.

The Archetype of Abundance and Subtle Economy

The evolutionary movement of consciousness is geared towards making better and better representations of the archetypes. For the economy and businesses, it means focusing not only on material profits but also on abundance in the subtle sector. One country, Bhutan, is already doing this; they have introduced the index of people's well-being to supplement gross national product as economic indicator.

This leads us to the question: can the subtle itself be the part of the economy? Engaging capitalism in the material sector in the past few centuries has generated unprecedented material wealth. Can engaging capitalism in the subtle sector similarly bring subtle abundance, even material abundance?

Can we build a subtle economy? There are people of gift in this sector, no doubt; but is there need? There is. Maslow's hierarchy of needs says when our material needs are satisfied, we hunger to satisfy our higher subtle needs, we turn from bare survival to increasing well-being. If you are one of those whose lower chakra survival needs are satisfied, it is apropos for you to pay attention to the higher chakra needs and potentialities. Needs for noble feelings, new meanings, and soul-building via archetypal explorations (fig. 22). If you don't, you will not find satisfaction with your life. Interestingly, as we shift our attention from the lower chakras (the first and the second) to the higher chakras, uncollapsed energies rise up and collapse in the three higher chakras with self-identity, helping to open them wide. This is what reduces the lower needs that Maslow suggested.

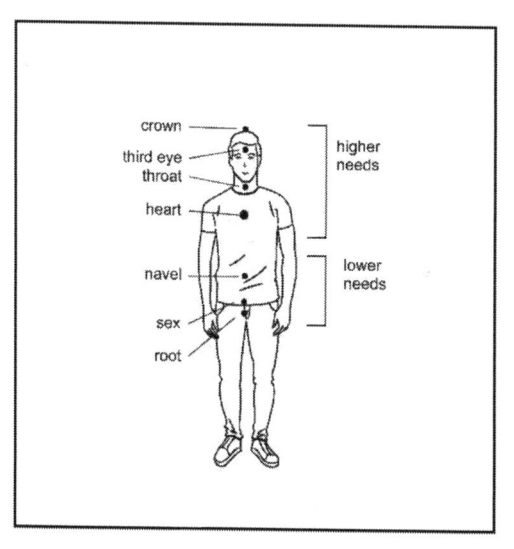

fig. 22: How Maslow's Lower needs and higher needs relate to the chakras

Actually, we already have a bit of a subtle economy: buying and selling meaning. Books, entertainment, meaning education (when done as business as it could and should) are examples.

It is not that hard to think of vital energy products. Homeopathy is an example of transferring healing energy from a poisonous medicinal plant to water and using that to heal people.

Let me give you another example. Can the energies of love be sold and bought as part of an economy? Quantum economics says yes. We can transform a human being through the creative process of inner creativity to embody love. By just sitting with this transformed person, you can experience the energy of love for a time that can heal you, make you feel positive, inspire you out of your depression. It would be cheaper than Prozac to be sure. There have been doctors who heal this way.

To produce the transformed people in bulk, we have to use inner creativity in an unprecedented scale. Is that feasible? This is the challenge of our age like building the first airplane was for another age. I think it can be done. We have the know-how and even a few prototypes. Accordingly, my friends and I are in the business of transforming people; we have established a university of transformative education in India as a business institution for soul making.

What happens when business people sell subtle products or produce human capital that emanates subtle products? Everyone knows that in order to succeed a businessperson must know his product better; so, he starts exploring. In this way, a subtle business transforms a businessperson from transaction to transformation. The businessperson now explores abundance with goodness and love and achieves real wealth, that quenches greed and brings satisfaction.

VI
The Archetypes of Abundance and Power: Is it Possible to Eliminate Elitism?

What is power? Power gives a can-do feeling in our gut in the same way as abundance can remove anal retentivity. Power also reflects a know-how—the knowledge that I can solve a problem, for example. But of course, people don't bring their can-do spirit to manifest things in the same way, everyone's conceptualization of power is not the same. So, power is an archetype transcending both its vital and mental representations.

Initially, we explore power for ourselves and use it to expand the domain of "our" power. The Jungian archetype for this kind of power is the Greek God Zeus (fig. 23a). When power is used not to empower ourselves but also to empower others, when we explore the archetype of power along with the archetype of goodness or love, the archetype appears as the Indian goddess Durga (fig. 23b). When power is engaged with love, it slays the instinctual animality in us, even the evil (*asura* in Sanskrit) in us.

Fig. 23 (a) The archetype of raw power is the Greek God Zeus.

fig. 23 (b) When power is explored with love, the archetype of power appearsin the representation of the divine mother, the Indiangoddess Durga, for example.

One important aspect of thequantum worldview is that it enables us to develop a theory of the well- documented phenomenonof reincarnation. An analysis of reincarnation shows that initially all humans are dominated by conditioning (*tamas* in Sanskrit), and it takes a few incarnations to catch on to the nuance for creative exploration. Obviously, without the direct experience of something new, a human being gets his or her ideas from others, in which case he or she better have a defined place in the society suitable for a follower. As one learns to be creative, the archetypes are explored in two stages.

The first stage involves using situational creativity (*rajas* in Sanskrit)—creativity staying within already known representations of archetypes. This is the level of creativity engaged in by businesspeople who explore abundance and politicians who explore the archetype of power. You can discern this by noting the empire-building tendency of these groups. Businesspeople have a lot of *tamas* and some *rajas*. Politicians tend to have more pure *rajas*.

People of *rajas* will dispense justice selectively because this helps them to expand their own power. The higher stage of creativity involves the use of fundamental creativity (*sattva* in Sanskrit) when meaning is explored in an expanded arena including new representations of the archetypes themselves. Only when a human being has arrived at the quality of relatively pure *sattva*, the archetype of power has already been explored by him or her, and there is not much selfish interest in it. Thus, it was that Plato suggested in his book on politics, *Utopia,* that only the people of predominant *sattva* with only a modicum of *rajas* should serve as heads of state, as benevolent dictators; their benevolence coming from their attention to the archetypes of justice and goodness. Only then would there be a dispensation of justice with even-handedness.

What does the arrival of democracy mean in this scenario? That human beings at all levels are ready or will soon be ready to explore creativity. Political power, instead of being concentrated in a few, ought to be shared with all people. In order for that to happen, political leaders today have to use their power to empower people first. For example, lift them from being merely followers. But you can use power in this way only if you have lost interest in hoarding it, that is, only if you have a preponderance of *sattva*. America was fortunate; its founding fathers, men like Thomas Jefferson were men of predominant *sattva* and they were listened to. This did not happen in India in spite of Mahatma Gandhi, nor in South Africa in spite of Nelson Mandela. These great moral leaders were just ignored in the subsequent facsimile of democracy that followed them. And Brazil, Russia, China and other developing countries have not been so fortunate as to have even one sattvic leader as a founder.

By and large, the progress of democracy has been slow in all nations because people of *rajas*, then and now have dominated the political scene. People of a modicum of *sattva* to keep the *rajas* in balance (Abe Lincoln, Franklin Roosevelt, Lalbahadur Sastri, and Atal Bihari Vajpayee, are a few examples) have been relatively rare.

Under scientific materialism, power has passed from people of predominant *rajas* to people of predominant *tamas* with only a modicum of *rajas* and no *sattva*; hence the dominance of businessmen in politics making the situation worse.

People of *tamas* and *rajas* use power to dominate others. Hence, the misuse of power today. There are threats of dictatorship everywhere.

If we depend on reincarnation alone to move people up gradually on the ladder of these qualities called *gunas* (*tamas*, *rajas*, and *sattva*), we are stuck with a simple hierarchy. Without a lot of reincarnations, it would seem impossible todevelop *rajas* and *sattva* that move people up the ladder of political leadership. But now that we understand the creativeprocess, thanks to the quantum worldview, I really think thatthe situation can change quickly. Many more people will engage inner creativity to help their outer creativity and hasten the process of moving up the ladder of *gunas* and someof them surely will come to politics and power and change the current scenario for the better.

VII
The Archetype of Love

I love these lines from a Joni Mitchell song: *I've looked at love/from both sides now/from up and down/but still somehow/it's love's illusions I recall/I really don't know love at all.*

I mentioned romantic love before that is a built-in capacity that we all have at the heart chakra. So, we fall in love and what happens? We really do experience love in the way it should be: we literally include the other in consciousness so much that we can give up our lives for our romantic partner. But after a while, be it few months or a few years, where does that love go? And thus, we wonder, Is love illusory? Is love an illusion after all?

Another example. Mothers have built-in circuits for motherly all-inclusive love. But children grow up and develop their individuality. When they don't reciprocate mother's love, mothers too tend to think, "Is love illusion?"

Okay, we can think in a better, more scientific way. Our brain is part of all this built-in capacity to love. When we love—romantic or motherly—these circuits are activated and love is effortless. And brain nurtures the love with neurochemicals and hormones for a period. And then it quits; especially when there is no reciprocation. We get disappointed.

Is there any way to do better? Yes, there is. It begins when we realize that love is an archetype. We cannot in this human body represent love in its suchness; all our love circuits are built from vital and mental representations. Representations are conditional. When the conditions change, the old representations are of little use. This is what happens repeatedly to us throughout our lives producing much agony and the misperception that love is illusory.

Can we love unconditionally? What prevents us? These are the questions for the exploration of love using fundamental creativity. When these questions are answered through quantum leaps and we manifest those answers in living, love is not illusory any more.

VIII
Good and Evil: the two Faces of the Archetype of Goodness

To most of our minds, the concept of ethics is a battle of good and evil. To be ethical is to side with good and to keep the evil at bay.

The idea of good and evil is built into us via the collective unconscious. Our ancestors, in a past era when group consciousness reigned humanity but the rational mind was gradually entering the picture, divided things up this way. We have instinctual feelings—violence, fear that contracts us—rational mind called them evil; we also have the capacity of love that expands our consciousness. Rational mind called this good. Prevalent nonlocal tribal consciousness of those ancient times made this part of humankind's nonlocal memory, the stuff of collective unconscious.

Religions realized that the built-in evil tendencies far outweigh our tendencies to be good. So, they invented the concept of sin and punishment to keep people ethical. You go to hell after you die if you are unethical, if you commit sin. So, you suppress and repress your evil tendencies. Religious ethics—goodness--is repression of evil.

Most religions put sex for pleasure in the category of evil; big mistake. When modern science came along, and people discovered another way to interpret the world according to the dictum of both theory and experimental data, ideals like hell soon bit the dust. The scientific mind challenged the idea that sex for pleasure is evil; pleasure feels good. So, the dictum of ethic became: evil is repression of goodness. Remove the repression; build a permissive society. Ethics will shine through.

Neither position worked very well to keep people ethical. Further confusion came when scientific materialism challenged the concept of archetypes altogether. The need for ethics became dubious.

The science of the brain created more confusion. Our brain on the average has five times more negative than positive tendencies. It is natural for the human being to be negative, to side with evil if you insist on that language.

All this changes with the quantum worldview. Nonlocal consciousness is the ground of being; we are all potentially one. And the evolutionary movement of consciousness is designed to take us there. So, ethics is a welcome step towards that end.

That does not make ethics easy. Nature of the brain dictates we have more negative built in us than positive. We have to transform, explore archetypes like goodness and love and embody them in order to balance good and evil in us.

We also have to recognize that transformation is a choice, not compulsory. To protect society and its people from unethical behaviour, in the interim we have to depend on laws.

If you are ignorant and choose to ignore ethics, it is the duty of the society and culture to teach you and persuade you about the oneness, about the archetype of goodness, about how to directly investigate this archetype through your creativity, etc. In other words, ethics must be emphasized in psychological education.

IX
The Archetype of Beauty

Creative truth may not come with absolute perfection, but it comes with beauty. And likewise, beauty comes with truth. The poet John Keats said, "Truth is beauty, beauty truth." Another poet, Rabindranath Tagore, wrote, "Beauty is truth's smile when she beholds her own face in a perfect mirror." If the authenticity of a creative insight cannot quite be judged on its truth value, which is bound to be relative, at least it can be judged by its beauty.

Physicist Paul Dirac, one of the early architects of quantum physics, discovered a mathematical equation that predicts the existence of antimatter, material stuff that annihilates regular matter on contact. At the time, there was no reason to believe that such a thing existed, but Dirac was guided by a keen sense of beauty. Wrote he, "It seems that if one is working from the point of view of getting beauty in one's equations, and if one has really a sound insight, one is on a sure line of progress." Indeed, Dirac's prediction came true a few years later in the form of the discovery of antiparticles. Even bulk antimatter has been isolated recently (2011) using CERN's supercollider machine.

A legend about the medieval Bengali poet Jaidev makes a similar point. Jaidev was in the middle of writing a scene in his masterpiece *Gita Govinda* in which "God-incarnate" Krishna is trying to appease his angry consort Radha. An inspired line of great beauty came to the poet's mind, and he wrote it down. But then he had second thoughts--Krishna is God incarnate, how could Krishna say such a human thing. So he crossed the line out and went for a walk. The legend is that while the poet was gone, Krishna himself came and resurrected the line. So great is the power of beauty in creative acts.

But what is beauty? Who judges it? Some authors try to find intellectual, emotional, or sociocultural causes for aesthetic experience; some say beauty is experienced intellectually by seeing order and harmony where ordinary people see chaos. Yet it is a truism that beauty is in the eyes of every beholder, the creative person just sees it better. Dirac put it well when he said, "Well--you feel it. Just like beauty in a picture or beauty in music. You can't describe it, it's something--and if you don't feel it, you just have to accept you are not susceptible to it. No one can explain it to you." When you feel it, your consciousness expands, enabling inclusivity.

This is why aesthetics—the Art of expanding consciousness with beautiful things around. This is why architecture too; particular forms of nature—either crystalline or living—are invitations to the archetypes.

When Pythagoras defined beauty as "the reduction of many to one," he was speaking of a very personal, transcendent creative experience of choice from the many-splendored quantum possibilities of an archetype. The poet Khalil Gibran said the same thing:

> And beauty is not a need but an ecstasy
> It is not a mouth thirsting nor an empty hand stretched forth,
> But rather a heart enflamed and a soul enchanted.
> It is not the image you would see nor the song you would hear,
> But rather an image you see though you
> close your eyes and a song you hear though you shut your ears.
> It is not the sap within the furrowed bark,
> nor a wing attached to a claw,
> But rather a garden for ever in bloom and
> a flock of angels for ever in flight.

X
The Archetype of Justice

Along with the archetype of goodness, social ethics must also serve the archetype of justice—that everyone should have the opportunity to explore and fulfil human potential. Justice is also about fairness—people should be treated equitably.

The archetype of justice is often portrayed as a blind lady with a measuring balance in hand; who is right and who is wrong must be judged with pure objectivity. What is forgotten in this depiction is fairness; is it fair to judge everyone on the same scale? It is like the idea of taxing everyone on the same percentage basis which is objective but not fair. How to get fairness in the equation for justice? Combine justice with love.

Democracy came about in some parts of the world in the eighteenth century as a huge example of creativity in the service of justice. Unfortunately, some parts of the world have still to catch up with that idea. The political movements in parts of the Middle East labelled as the Arab Spring was a good creative beginning in the right direction or so it seemed; but now with the rise of terror groups much of that region is moving backwards in history towards the religious elitism of the past.

In the past century, we have done good in parts of the world in administering justice: today, women's rights, coloured people's rights, and even homosexual rights are being acknowledged in many parts of the world. In America, justice is demanding (through such movements as Occupy Wall Street, black life matters, and me-too) that everyone should have the opportunity to fulfil the American dream. But these movements are being followed by a huge backlash. The same thing is happening in India. We make some progress in eliminating discrimination against lower castes, we fall behind again.

Finally, one reason we have fallen behind manifesting justice, not only in America but all around the world, is that we try to do it through laws established via mechanical situational problem solving, not by genuine acts of creativity. Agreed: Laws are necessary to protect the innocent. Women have long been subjected to sexual harassment and date rape on co-ed campuses. Campus administrators have done very little to address the needs of these traumatized women until very recently. Moreover, perpetrators have rarely been prosecuted in criminal courts but rather in campus tribunals where they received little more than a slap on the hand! Better legal protection is needed no doubt.

But we must also recognize the importance of transformational education. Requiring incoming freshmen to participate in sensitivity training – for instance, to truly understand what constitutes consent—is a good step. But why stop there? In quantum science, we have scientific ideas pertaining to relationships that could help every young person to navigate this difficult arena.

Trying to protect women with legality alone will only end up putting a damper on non-rational romantic behaviour. We need all the prongs: legality, sensitivity training, and transformational education using the quantum worldview to ensure that justice is served.

XI
The Archetype of Wholeness and Healthcare in A Quantum Society

As humans we live many dichotomies: conditioning-creativity dichotomy, inner-outer dichotomy, male-female dichotomy, good-evil dichotomy, these are only a few of the dichotomies we live. Wholeness is the archetype we explore to become whole integrating these dichotomies and others that divide us.

In general, being divided is suffering, and healing is restoring wholeness. But human cultures everywhere have forgotten this.

Healthcare via allopathy is now so mechanical and the insurance system works in such a way that family doctors often make their money by performing unnecessary tests for patients rather than from treating them. In other words, they may as well be replaced by robots that can say "hello" equally well.

Okay, I am joking, but just a little. Doctors are intelligent people as concerned about this trend of medicine as anyone else. Many doctors choose to be surgeons and emergency care physicians; they would rather have stress than the boredom of the regular profession.

All this changes with integrative medicine when medicine becomes a healing science once again with a theory to boot, and we go back to healing and exploring wholeness as the purpose of a health professional.

As healing becomes a science of wholeness, thanks to the quantum worldview, the current domination of the field by the pharmaceutical research and insurance companies will stop. Many of the sophisticated mechanical information-oriented details of medical training will give way to the systematic simplicity that a theoretical understanding of healing would bring to the profession. Instead, medical professionals will explore vital energies, sensitivity toward intuition, and pay attention to their own wholeness creatively as they explore their profession. Only then restoring wholeness in patients via creative exploration—quantum healing—will become practical. Healers literally will collaborate with patients in the creative exploration of quantum healing of all kinds of difficult disease.

Healthcare—Mental Health

Mental health, or rather emotional/mental health, will be one of the much sought-after professions of the quantum society. This is because (1) people's concept of abundance willinclude mental health; and (2) education will include building inner character and transformation that will require expansive teacher education in mental health.

One of the interesting new discoveries of the quantum worldview is the induction effect that the presence of a person established in nonlocal consciousness creates. Right now, our treatment of psychosis is limited to those cases where allopathic medicine can keep the patient under manageable conscious control. Using the phenomenon of induction, however, a therapist can use various alternative subtle energy therapies as well.

A major application of this will happen in dealing with criminals. Today, we have prison ashram projects with a reasonable amount of success in maintaining peace and harmony in a prison. With the use of the induction technique and therapy supplementing the prison ashram projects, it should be possible to rehabilitate even hard-corecriminals—sociopaths and psychopaths.

Wholeness and Politicians

Politicians should pay attention to the archetype of wholeness. Today, with worldview polarization, compromise with truth, and dealing with me-centredness, a politician's life is full of conflicts because of a lack of congruence between how she thinks, how she projects herself to voters, how she lives, and how she handles her profession, for example fundraising. These conflicts produce stress, and stress causes dissatisfaction and eventual burnout among other things. A way out is to seriously invoke the creative exploration of the archetype of wholeness using the process of quantum creativity.

The Dichotomy of Sacred and Mundane

Then there is also the dichotomy of sacred—spirituality--and the mundane, the ordinary. Ever since human beings discovered the archetypes, they have separated the inner exploration of the archetypes as sacred activity as opposed to mundane activities of ordinary living and even outer explorations of feeling and meaning involving the archetypes. Like all other dichotomies, this one too has produced much suffering.

When the ultimate goal of spirituality is defined as the self-archetype, the sacred-mundane dichotomy continues unabated. The enlightened do not see any dichotomy between themselves and the ordinary people. Nevertheless, because enlightened people live in Oneness much of the time, people worship them and impose sacredness on them.

Does the exploration of the archetype of wholeness also bridge this stubborn dichotomy? It does. In quantum science, we define a new kind of spirituality—quantum spirituality—the exploration of the archetype of wholeness as our goal until and unless we tire of living itself. The goal is to develop a society without any dichotomy, any conflict arising from dichotomy.

XII
The Archetypes of Love, Wholeness, and Self

Is love the most fundamental archetype and the most important archetype of all? It is certainly the most ubiquitous, universal archetype that we all pursue, that we all need to pursue. There are three basically fundamental *archetypes to explore in order to change the ways we are built*. And it is very important to see which those three are. One is love. And another one is the "self" archetype. And there is a third one that also is very important. That is the "wholeness" archetype. Love is the most attractive one, and most people see the necessity of investigating love very early on. Good thing too. When we are able to combine our embodiment of power with love, we can share our power with others; we can empower others using our power. When we combine our seeking abundance with love, we find abundance and develop the capacity to share. In this way, we rise beyond elitism.

As we grow psychologically, we get into the archetype of wholeness. Initially, when we lack wholeness, when we get sick, we just look at the illness as a sort of suffering. We look at it as an inconvenience. We go to the doctor and we just want her to cure us. I don't mind if the doctor gives me some pills or just finds a quick fix and that's it. But at some stage of our developing maturity, we recognize that the cure is not the same as healing. Curing a disease does not necessarily put us into ease. At that point we become interested in health as wholeness; health not only at the level where I don't suffer but also at the level where I want to optimize my wellbeing, my wholeness. Then I am already exploring the archetype of wholeness.

Some people, maybe we all sooner or later, get bored with all these activities, creative as they maybe. This state, called *Vairagya* in Sanskrit, prompts us to see the importance of the "self" archetype, "who am I?" As we investigate, the first thing that occurs to us is the limitations of the *ego* I/me. And then we ask the question, "Is this all there is or can I overcome the limitations of this I/me'?" Eventually that leads us to the journey of self-realisation, the doorway to the fifth layer of human existence.

If love, wholeness, and the self-archetypes are fundamental, crucial archetypes, how come those archetypes are not playing a part in everything? Well, throughout our recent history we just have missed the importance of these *archetypes* in two ways: First of all, we had a religious worldview in which we falsely interpreted the archetype of wholeness and opted for something that is not wholeness. Look at what religions do. They divide the world into spiritual and material. So, it is the flip side of the materialist mistake. They make the same mistake, ignoring half of our wholeness, our outer wellbeing. The materialist chooses the material representation of abundance. The spiritualist chooses the spiritual representation of abundance, but neither of them remembers wholeness. Of course, we are not doing too badly because the spiritual worldview has guided us for thousands of years and some good has come out of that. Four hundred years ago, when modern science came onto the scene, we made a compromise. And it was very holistic. Under what is called the philosophy of modernism, we valued matter and mind, spirituality and materiality, combining into a viable worldview albeit in a dualistic way—mind and matter, separate. But for a while, we were exploring the archetype of wholeness. And indeed modernism, that worldview, gave us institutions of democracy, capitalism, liberal education, which have enormous impact in developing human civilization. The Quantum Worldview is nothing but an integrated form of modernistic dualism. Some people call it transcendent modernism, *transmodernism* for short. All we have done is, integrated the dualistic partners, mind and matter of modernism, within consciousness. Unfortunately, instead of going from modernism directly into the quantum worldview, we took the sidetrack to scientific materialism, and that was a very unfortunate mistake for humanity.

XIII
See the World as a Vale for Soul-making

The title of this section is borrowed from a romantic poet of the eighteenth century, John Keats who wrote to a friend thus. Evolution has given those of us who have penetrated the material sheath into the vital and mental sheath the next task—soul making, making representations of the archetypes in our body and brain in the process making ourselves into soulful beings.

To do this it is important that we sublimate coiled up vital *kundalini* energy at the root and sex chakra all the way to the sixth brow chakra. People of outer creativity do that to some extent. They have so much sexual energy that although they mostly dissipate it via sex, most often, somewhat unconsciously, the excess energy rises to the sixth brow chakra. Freud knew about it; he called this transformed sexual energy *libido* in some of his later writings. So did Wilhelm Reich who called this transformed sexual energy *orgone*.

In India, they have mythologized the kundalini rising all the way to brow chakra before being collapsed in the myth of Siva burning the god of love, *Madan*, who plays the same role as cupid in the West. Siva is a yogi in this myth, always meditates. But a young and beautiful girl Parvati has fallen for him, and every day she comes and sits with Siva. Siva, of course, pays no attention. One day, when Madan is passing by, sees the girl's frustration of unrequited love, and takes kindly to the girl. He throws the arrow of romantic love at Siva, Siva's concentration breaks, and his kundalini coiled up all this time rises to the brow and collapses all at once. The chakra becomes so hot, it bursts into flame and the fire burns Madan to ashes.

The story has a good ending. Now that Siva's concentration is broken, he does notice Parvati. And eventually, the two become lovers.

What happens when the sixth chakra opens like this? It is said that the opening makes room for intuitive thinking in addition to rational thinking. This is referred to as the opening of the third eye—which St. Buenaventura in the West called the eye of contemplation. Our cognitive facility before consisted of sensory perception of stimuli sent by the physical world plus cognition by feeling or sensory perception and cognition by thinking. Now there is second avenue: we receive stimuli from consciousness via intuition and cognize them via feeling and thinking.

And more. When the 6th chakra opens fully, then not only the door of intuition opens but also we regain something that we lost with the development of the neocortex and the self of mentation there. Animals in the form of pets feel instinctual energy in their mid-brain; so, there is self-identity there for them. With the development of the thinking-self in us humans, this mid-brain self is totally suppressed. With full kundalini sublimation, we regain the use of the mid-brain self and that translates as a control of hypothalamus and amygdala, and the hormones in the body. In this way such a person can now totally control the negative emotional brain circuits which means they have complete emotional intelligence. This is in addition to the intuitive intelligence. Together with opening of the heart and the navel, and balancing and harmonizing all the four selves is what Aurobindo called supramental intelligence.

When all these openings of the 6th chakra is used to embody the archetypes via fundamental creativity and living the insights it brings us, we have completed soul making.

Living in the soul level is wonderful but we still live in the vital-mental layers except for occasional forays in the supramental when we intuit or have a creative insight. In the absence of memory making of the archetypes in suchness in our physical body, we cannot stabilize living in the supramental layer.

But we can live in the fifth layer. You will see. This is the subject of the next two chapters.

XIV
How is it like Living as a soul?

In outer creativity involving science, we access the archetypes momentarily when we take the quantum leap. But when we manifest the insight it is mostly the job of the rational mind. In all my early life as a scientist of outer creativity, I experiencedflow only once.

It is different in the realm of art and music though. We all have seen musicians go into flow. The famous Ravi Shankar once gave a performance in Eugene where I live. He did not want to stay in a hotel; so, the organizers arranged for him to stay in my house. I was expecting to have engaging chats with him, but no such luck. He and his associates practiced the whole time.

You know why. Mastery takes us to confidence and confidence enables us to relax opening the door for the quantum self. So when in that relaxed state of mastery over the material, we create music (or engage in art), we fall into the quantum self often and get inspired with new insights, small they may be, come back to the repertoire of the ego to give form to the inspiration, and so on and so forth. This is flow.

There is flow in dancing too. Back in 1983, I once went to a workshop to learn how to open my chakras to experience feelings in the body. So open became I that on the very last evening celebration, I surprised myself. There was a very accomplished dancer in our group of twenty-six, and everyone was coaxing her to dance one last time as a parting gift to us. She was playing coy. So, I spoke up. "If you dance, I will give up all my inhibitions about disciplined dancing and try my best to match you step for step. Now, will you dance with me?"

She agreed. And fear gripped me. Why did I offer to do this stupid thing, volunteering for something that I had never succeeded in doing, the few times I had tried? I once enrolled in an Arthur Murray dance class to learn the Foxtrot, Waltz, Tango, and all that stuff. One by one the dance teachers tried to teach me the steps, I could not learn even one dance. So, they gave up and taught me the barest minimum, the basic rock and roll, completely undisciplined letting go. That was my entire dance repertoire. (It still is!) And me! Dancing with this accomplished dancer? No way!

Yes way! I went to the stage and surrendered. Relaxation came. And I danced, matching the dancer step for step; or rather I should say my feet danced while I watched. That was flow.

When I got into inner creativity and discovered for myself the insight that took me to unconditional love (read my book *Quantum Spirituality* written with Valentina Onisor for details), the manifestation stage of the insight had many instances of flow.

So, although I am just a novice in soul-making, this is my hypothesis: people at this level live more and more in flow.

What do they do to increase flow time? They take on a multiple of archetypes to explore. They engage in outer creativity—writing, art, music. No worries. Their outer is integrated with the inner. They won't fall back into outer exclusively, never again.

Are there role models for this? It is hard to find role models in the Western culture or in any culture right now; in the past though, the American poet Walt Whitman comes to mind. I am a devotee of three such people all of whom lived in the 19-20th centuries: Rabindranath Tagore, Mahatma Gandhi, and Sri Aurobindo.

Chapter 9
Who am I? The Two Faces of the Self

I
The Ego: How the Self Acquires I—me Polarity

The layer of unlimited joy is the abode of the quantum self, our real I, not the I/me that we usually experience, that we call the ego. Of course, the biggest barrier to accept the idea of the quantum self for most people is that they experience on a regular basis only the ego. Ego is the biggest barrier to getting out of the human condition of limitations because its nature is to maintain a status quo, a control that it feels it must retain over its affairs. How does this ego arise if our initial response to every external stimulus should be the quantum self?

The details of ego development are beyond the scope of this book but I will give you a quick summary. Quantum measurement produces memory; reflection in the mirror of memory produces conditioning, tendencies to act that we call our habit patterns and character traits; the use of our ability to revisit our memories again and again and reconstructing them gives us personalized programmes that constitute our personality. In this way we get a second pole of the self-experience that I call ego-character-persona or simply "me," since the "I" tend to become implicit in this state.

In this way we develop our simple hierarchical ego/character/persona of everyday experience with "I" virtually becoming implicit; this is what we all refer to as I/me or just "me." And who can blame me for this illusory construction? The "I" that I experience is one that I can introspect and make into me; add to this the fact that I am deciding which behaviour of my conditioned spectrum of behaviour I will choose (for example I choose the flavour of ice cream I want given a choice and consciousness is benevolent, it goes along with my choice!) and thirdly, I choose whatever personality mask I want to wear in a giving situation.

II
The Importance of Intuition as a Conduit for Experiencing the Quantum Self

In our ego, we tend to get detached from the unity consciousness. The detachment is more or less complete for psychopaths and sociopaths, but even normal people, especially the intellectuals among them, live in so much contraction of consciousness, that for them oneness-of-consciousness talk is humbug. An example. Freud was no stranger to "oceanic" feelings of oneness. But he rationalized, these must be feelings of infantile helplessness. Similarly, the materialist rationalizes, Consciousness is nothing but annoying subjective qualia of experiences.

Still! One question that always has bothered me is this: Is the quantum self-experience as rarefied as mystics claim? Sure, the creative experience especially the spiritual experience of *samadhi*, historically speaking has been pretty rare. But no doubt you notice that as we have begun to understand the creative process behind these experiences more people are reporting having the creative quantum leap—a state of insight that is a pretty good facsimile of a *samadhi*. It also has become clear that both creative and spiritual experiences begin with an experience that we call intuition. An intuition experience is always a quantum self-experience since archetypes are forever new to us.

How do we experience intuitions? Let me repeat. No memory making, no tangled hierarchy, no actualization. For the actualization, we can go to the mental route; a mental representation is made (in possibility) of the archetypal possibility; when this mental meaning is sifted through the brain's tangled hierarchy, we get to an actualization of an archetypal experience. But only if we have the requisite sensitivity to intuitions. When actualization takes place, the mental meaning along with the original intuition, actualizes. How do we know? The actualization of the archetypal object of intuition gives us an uneasiness that something special happened that we should follow through. This is because archetypal experiences always come with truth-value. The realisation that there is truth in this vaguely formed intuitive thought is what makes us uneasy.

In this way, there is nothing rarefied about the quantum self. If one develops a sensitivity to intuition, quantum self can be everybody's everyday phenomenon. And believe it! Some people live this way. This is why we find them always inspired.

How to develop such sensitivity to intuitions? Actually, here the wisdom traditions—even many religions—are way ahead of the scientists who still struggle to include intuitions in their belief system. Scientific materialism is a harsh mistress. The wisdom traditions' prescription is meditation. Meditation relaxes us; slows us down. Brain wave measurements show that when our brain is in the beta mode (brain wave frequency of 13.5-35 Hz), we are thinking and concentrating on our thought because our tasks require it. When we relax, the brain is in the slow wave mode of alpha (7.5-13.5 Hz) and theta (3.5-7.5 Hz). It takes a while to develop the necessary relaxed awareness, but this is when it is likely we can fall into the quantum-self and have the awareness of intuitions. So, it is a little paradoxical, isn't it? Relaxed awareness is a prerequisite to an experience that neuroscience has discovered is accompanied by gamma bursts of frequency over 40 Hz. Why gamma burst? Because there is a heightened state of awareness and cognition in the intuitive or insightful experience.

There is also an affective quality of archetypal experiences, the reason we call our intuitions as sometimes giving us a "gut feeling" or a feeling in the heart; gut and heart refer to chakra points. The reason we know: archetypes can not only be represented in the mind as mental meaning but also as feeling of the energy of vital movement at the chakra points of the morphogenetic/liturgical blueprints for the functioning of an organ at the chakra. In this way developing sensitivity to feelings always helps increase our sensitivity to intuition.

Do women have more intuition because they are more sensitive to feeling, much more than men who are mainly thought-centred? You bet; it is no joke. Women are more sensitive to their feelings in the body; so, they are aware of their intuition more often than not. That's what makes the difference.

III
Is the Holy Spirit a Fantasy of the Religious Mind?

One of the most harmful legacy of the current science based on scientific materialism is the systematic undermining that has taken place about the importance of intuition in our everyday life. (And emotions, too, but to a lesser degree thanks to the female half of humanity.) In the ancient times and cultures intuition was recognized as "talking to God," or as summons from the Holy Spirit. Creative people of those old cultures knew that an intuition is an invitation from the archetypes of value from the transcendent domain of reality and they followed up the invitation with the exploration of the archetype. This is how our civilization has progressed. The exploration of the archetypes has led to the great arts (the exploration of the archetype of beauty) and the spiritual traditions (the exploration of the archetypes of self, truth, love, and goodness), to human laws and justice systems (the exploration of the archetype of justice), to economics and business (the exploration of the archetype of abundance), to politics (the exploration of the power archetype) to the healing sciences (the exploration of the archetype of wholeness), and more recently, even natural science (the exploration of the archetype of truth), institutions that form the foundation of civilization. In our inner landscape, the psyche, the exploration of the goodness and beauty archetypes has given us moral and aesthetic development respectively of impressive proportions.

A few years back, Bill O'Reilly, then a prominent Fox News persona was speaking to a TV journalist who was interviewing him about his new book *Killing Jesus* (or maybe about one of O'Reilly's other books of the "killing" series). The journalist asked, "Where did your idea of the name of this series of books come from?" To this O'Reilly said, "from the Holy Spirit." This response then became the butt of a Steven Colbert joke whose show is where I picked up the story.

I am sure a Fox News audience would not have been amused with Colbert's treatment of O'Reilly's comment. For them, O'Reilly is just reporting fact. But it is a joke for Colbert and his liberal audience because many liberals today under the aegis of scientific materialism are sceptic of concepts such as the Holy Spirit let alone admit that an experience of Holy Spirit is even possible. In this way, these liberals undermine the importance of intuition.

But intuition is the doorway to creativity—both outer exploration and inner transformation. When intuition is undervalued civilization itself stops progressing. And more. Ordinary people lose their way to balancing the negative with positive and find even temporary wholeness.

Back to the liberal reaction to Bill O'Reilly. These liberals are not entirely without reason to react negatively to concepts such as God or Holy Spirit. Under pop religion, for example under the religion of popular Christianity of Fox News aficionados, God or Holy Spirit are also conceived as nonmaterial entities separate from you, and authoritarian to boot. In this scientific age, why should anyone pay heed to the authority of a nonmaterial other even if such existed?

Torn between a rock and a hard place, are we? We don't have to be. Eastern religions—such as Hinduism, Taoism, and Buddhism—conceives of God as a non-ordinary state of consciousness and the Holy Spirit as a deep self beyond ego. And now we have discovered the science behind the concept.

An aside. Buddhist teachings have a subtlety that may initially confuse you. They call this deep self as *no self.* However, as you have seen in the pages above, the concept of no self can be accommodated in our new science of self also as the quantum self. So, this entity of different names is not really separate from you; it is you, it is just not ordinarily accessible.

But admittedly, for many a Westerner, to follow Eastern religion is a hard thing to swallow—it is after all "foreign" stuff. Of course, many knowledgeable people of the West have long ago recognized that esoteric Christianity has the same message as the Eastern religions. Eastern concepts are not really foreign! Unfortunately, this is not common knowledge. Scientists and TV personalities like Steven Colbert can hardly be expected to have heard of esoteric Christianity.

And oh yes! O'Reilly and the Holy Spirit. Now that quantum physics validates the Holy Spirit as the quantum self, your view should change. When you process the full importance of what quantum physics is telling us about consciousness and our self, you won't need to laugh at people who mention Holy Spirit; instead, you might laugh at those who scoff at the mention of Holy Spirit!

IV
An Imaginary Dialog about the relation of I and Me

In February 2017, I was invited to speak at a conference in Kolkata, India, on consciousness and quantum physics where a philosopher named Bijoy Baruah presented a delightful paper on the relation of I and me. This dialogue grew out of my understanding of what he was trying to say.

Philosopher: In his imaginary book, *The world as I found it*, the great philosopher Ludwig Wittgenstein imagines creating a record of everything he finds in the world. But he never mentioned himself. Why? Because you never find "I" the subject in the world. Call it Swittgenstein.

Wittgenstein the object he certainly did find, that is his me, call it Twittgenstein. What is the relationship between Swittgenstein and Twittgenstein? Are they different or are they identical?

Scientist: Are you talking about the subject-object relationship as in grammar?

Philosopher: Well, the complication shows up even in grammar. Not in a sentence like *I love my dog*; there the relationship of I the subject, and the dog, the predicate is "agentive," the actor-object relationship fixes the direction to be one-way, from I to the dog; the relationship is a simple hierarchy.

But consider the sentence *I love myself*. Or better yet, *I love me*. Are I and me ontologically the same being? Grammatically it is okay; psychologically it is okay.

But yet, how can they be the same when me exists only because I exist? Isn't it the "eye" of the I that creates me? I look at myself and make it into a me by objectifying myself. Then are they ontologically different, are they different beings?

Scientist: I see what you are getting at. I agree; they are different. Look at the scientific mechanism that makes I into a me. It's the act of self-consciousness, it is the act of image making. In this way, me is a self-image, an appearance.

Philosopher (interrupting): An appearance to whom? To the I. I is the awareness, me is the appearance.

But something still bothers me. Suppose I ask, What am I? The answers, I am a philosopher, I am a lover, I am 5' 5" tall defines the person that I am. I am the owner of my personal characteristics including personas I have acquired. That defines me. What am I? I am me.

How is that possible? Surely, me and I are not interchangeable. Surely, an appearance cannot be interchanged with the authentic.

Scientist: There you are. If we define an authentic me without the self-image, just the character that I have acquired, then I can be me. As I add more elements to my character, I go on enriching me, the authentic me. And since I and me are both authentic, it does not matter that one is the subject and the other the object. The object continuously emerges from the subject. The distinction becomes unimportant for all practical purpose.

Philosopher: I agree. And to the extent that one's self-image is virtually invisible to me, if I am deeply into me, I see oneness of my subject-self and my object self. And this is the structured duality of subject and object that escapes most people, even philosophers who subscribe to scientific materialism.

Scientist: I have noticed.

Philosopher: And yet the structured duality does not have to be a matter of pure philosophy. I as subject can stay aloof from the me that I tend to become as I partake the bittersweet fruits of *Samsara*. You know if I maintain vigilance, via mindfulness meditation and all that, I can maintain independence from the me that is constantly being generated by I; what I do, think, feel, and all that. Maybe Wittgenstein did that and that's why he never found his I in all he experienced.

Scientist: Maybe. And I have good news for you. Quantum science is telling us that when the unity consciousness, the ground of being from which both subject and object arise, creates the manifest world by actualizing potentiality, the subject/self I it becomes has a tangled hierarchical relationship with the objects. And this "I" as quantum self has no previous memory to introspect and create its "me." We must concede it is a state of no-me.

It seems that this quantum self no-me I loves I/me (consciousness is benevolent); suppose the I/me reciprocates and develops a tangled hierarchical relationship with the quantum self I; when I becomes me and when the me becomes I and the relationship between them becomes truly blurred, then we—I and me--realize that we both arise from the One, we *are* One. And this love that we experience in this "flow" between I and me is not the usual dependent love, but a kind of "aloof" love.

Philosopher: Wonderful, wonderful.

Scientist: By the way, Wittgenstein may never have found his I, but mystics do and they discover that indeed it has no me. But you have to open the door of perception wide open to have the experience of no-me. This is one problem for Western philosophers and scientists. As a group, they don't meditate or *creatively* engage with the question, "Who am I? Am I different from me?" Only if you engage creatively, you get the surprise: there *is* an I with no-me.

V
Self Realisation: the penetration of the fourth Supramental Sheath

When *vairagya* hits, a state that the philosopher Franklin Merrell-Wolff called "high indifference," we explore the self archetype earnestly. The creative exploration of other archetypes does not satisfy any more; nothing does. There is only one thing to do: to get out of the game of birth-death-rebirth altogether. Hindus call this liberation and Buddhists have a similar concept of *Nirvana*–cessation of desire. The strategy consists of the exploration of the self-archetype. The creative process is the same, do-be-do-be-do; then insight.

However, the insight is subtle. We discover, there is no self. Self is not an archetype like other archetypes. Its embodiment—the quantum self—is no self but the doorway to unity consciousness itself.

The manifestation stage is also subtle. When we creatively discover the primary nature of the self, *I am the quantum self*, we are called self-realized: we know we are the quantum self, the ego is a secondary epiphenomenon. Why identify with the epiphenomenon when you know reality? Thus begins the journey of manifestation of killing the ego and making room for unmitigated quantum living.

I will give an analogy. Imagine you in your ego-identity are a salt figurine and taking a swim in the ocean. The salt figurine melts away; your ego-identity will dissolve in the ocean of unity consciousness, right?

So, after the dissolution of the ego-identity, who are you? Some people today bypass *vairagya* and explore self-realisation without proper preparation. They follow the creative process and have the aha-insight. What then? They want to enjoy the fruit of their insight which requires a strong ego! They do all kinds of egotistic things beginning with writing a book at once proclaiming their enlightenment.

When instead, you first earn your right to investigate the self archetype—detachment from accomplishments, and you go through the manifestation stage of creativity and identify with the quantum self, you have no place to stand on; quantum self is forever dynamic. Your ego is dissolved in the ocean of oneness, so you need to learn to spend much of your time in the wholeness of the ocean. This is part of the manifestation process of self-realisation. Is that possible? Isn't that living in the unconscious? How is it different from deep sleep then?

Chapter 10
The Fifth Layer: "Experiencing" the Unconscious in Suchness

I
Experiencing the Fifth Layer: *Nirvikalpa Samadhi*

Is it possible to "experience" the unconscious? One advantage is obvious. Then, we can directly verify the idea that consciousness is the ground of being by experiencing what is normally unconscious in us.

The prerequisite, in fact the doorway to such ontological states is to identify with the quantum self. When you have no place to stand on in conscious awareness where would you live but in the unconscious Oneness?

Savikalpa and Nirvikalpa Samadhi

In self-realisation, what one experiences is the oneness of everything, the subject, the object(s), the entire field of awareness, all seem to become one. In the yoga literature, this is called *savikalpa Samadhi* in Sanskrit; *samadhi* means the balance of the two poles of subject and object. *Savikalpa* means with separation. In other words, in this experience, we become aware of the dependent co-arising of the universal quantum self (subject) and the world (object). We do not expect to experience consciousness undivided from its possibilities. Any experience, by definition, involves actualization of possibility into actuality and subject-object split. In other words, *savikalpa samadhi* seems to be as deep (or high) aswe can go in experience.

Very confusingly to the rational mind, the Eastern spiritual literature refers to another kind of *samadhi* called *nirvikalpa samadhi*. The Sanskrit word *nirvikalpa* means without split-- without subject-object separation. If there is no experience without subject-object split, what does this Samadhi without subject-object split represent?

To understand this, consider deep sleep. In deep sleep, there is no subject-object split, and there is no experience. But there is no problem with accepting that we sleep either. We all sleep and it is an accepted state of consciousness. When we sleep, stimuli can bombard us, our brain in the unconscious can process the stimuli, but no actualization.

So *nirvikalpa samadhi* has to be understood as a sleep-like state in which some special unconscious processing takes place that is cognized only at the moment of waking. This is what the East Indian sage Patanjali meant when he said, "meditate on knowledge that comes during sleep." How is this possible? Quantum physics has the answer: delayed choice.

II
The Delayed-Choice Experiment in the Macro world

The original delayed-choice experiment was carried out with photons: our choice *after* what is supposed to be "fact" in Newtonian thinking affects the outcome. The macro world delayed choice experiment was carried out successfully by the physicist/parapsychologist Helmut Schmidt and his collaborators in 1993. It will not only reinforce your belief in the efficacy of conscious choice but also help you comprehend near-death phenomenon.

Schmidt's experiments involved random number generators, which generate random sequences of zeroes and ones using random radioactive decay products.

In his 1993 experiment, the radioactive decay was detected by electronic counters, resulting in the computer generation of random number sequences that were then recorded on floppy disks. It was all carried out unseen by human eyes, months ahead of the time that the psychics came into the experiment. The computer even made a printout of the scores and, with such utmost care that no observer saw it; the printout was sealed and sent to an independent researcher, who left the seals intact.

A few months later, the independent researcher instructed the psychics to try to influence the random numbers generated in a specific direction, to produce either more zeros or more ones. The psychics tried to influence the random number sequence in the direction proposed by the independent researcher. Only after they had completed this stage did the independent researcher open the sealed envelope to check the printout to see if there was a deviation in the direction instructed.

The researchers found a statistically significant effect; amazing, huh? Somehow the psychics were able to influence even a macroscopic printout of data that, according to conventional wisdom, had been taken months ago. The conclusion is inescapable: all objects remain in possibility, even macroscopic objects, until consciousness chooses from the possibilities and an event of collapse occurs. Then it all manifests, retroactively.

III
The State of Consciousness called *Turiya*

The nirvikalpa phenomenon now can be explained. Via an intention that aligns with cosmic intention, the adept falls into the unconscious and processes stimuli from the collective and the quantum unconscious. The mental cognition and memories thereof are processed (let's call them *imperience*) in potentiality. When the adept wakes up from the sleep like state, the delayed choice and collapse take place actualising not only the present moment but everything before it, all the imperiences that are causally connected.

What is the special vision that is revealed upon waking up from nirvikalpa? The mystic sage Swami Sivananda describes it thus:

> There are two kinds of . . . *nirvikalpa samadhi*. In the first the *gnyani* [wise explorer], by resting in Brahman (Sanskrit word for Consciousness), sees [processes] the whole world within himself as a movement of ideas, as a mode of being or a mode of his own existence .... This is the highest state of realisation. ...
>
> In the second variety the world vanishes from view and the *gnyani* rests on pure attributeless *Brahman*.

Clearly the first kind of nirvikalpa samadhi is the ultimate state of unconscious processing when the explorer processes pure consciousness attributes—quantum possibilities of ideas. This state of consciousness is called *Turiya* and the associated limitless *ananda* upon waking is given a special name *turiyananda*.

The explorer sees the entire world of quantum possibilities including the archetypes within himself and yet transcends it. It is not an experience but a state of consciousness that can only be experienced on a delayed basis using delayed choice, after one wakes up from the state.

Sivananda's second kind of *nivikalpa* state is a deeper state of non-experience in that it has no attribute—not even possibilities. The non-experience is called *Nirvana*—extinction of all desires. Buddhists call this state *Shunyat*a--nothingness. Hindus call it *nirguna Brahman*, Brahman without attributes. Hindus say that arriving here one gains liberation—*moksha*—liberation from death-birth-rebirth cycle. Christians call this state Godhead (prior to God).

One thing is certain: we can say nothing about this state. Very wisely, the philosopher Ludwig Wittgenstein said, "Whereof one cannot speak, thereof one must remain silent."

Are there actual people who live in *Nirvikalps*, literally with God?

Good question, the section heading. I told you earlier about my experience with Franklin Merrel-Wolff. He had his self realisation at the ripe age of 49. Soon after he entered *nirvikalpa samadhi* as well. Read his book, *Philosophy of Consciousness without an object*, very inspiring.

When I met him he was 97. I asked him if he still entered *nirvikalpa*; he said as he was getting older, it was enervating him too much, so he gave up.

In India, even as recently as in the twentieth century, we have plenty of examples of people who have entered *nirvikalpa*: Ramana Maharshi, Paramahansa Yogananda, Anandamayi Ma, Swami Sivananda, Jiddu Krishnamurti. Of this illustrious list, by all accounts, Ramana Maharshi and Anandamayi Ma spent much of their time every day in *nirvikalpa*. Devotees loved their company when they gave *darshan* after their *nirvikalpa*, they felt so happy.

How does one get into *nirvikalpa*? Is it a quantum leap? Does one go through the creative process every time they go into *nirvikalpa*?

Amazingly no. They intend (this is where it takes energy), and they just fall into the quantum self as no self and thereon to *nirvikalpa.* At the age of 16, Ramana was not an exceptional kid by anymeans. But one day, he was gripped by the fear of death. So, he did an experiment. He told himself to feign death; he stilled himself to immobility. "Now I am dead to the physical body." Then he made his vital energies and thoughts still. "Now my vital body and mind are dead." Then he intendedthat his soul is dead. To his surprise, he found that consciousness is still very much there and more luminous than ever. With this Nirvikalpa "experience", he was enlightened. Later, he was known to stay in *nirvikalpa* for hours; a devotee had to feed him.

How does mere intention accomplish the task? Anandamayi Ma had her first *nirvikalpa* at age 9. Clearly, both Ramana and Ma had a lot of practice in their past lives; they were ready.

IV
Why Enlightenment?

So, what is the point of all this talk of spiritual enlightenment that ends with a state about which you can say nothing?

There is a claim in the spiritual literature of India that people of *nirvikalpa* capacity are totally transformed, their identity completely shifts to the quantum self except when the ego is needed for everyday chores, for ego-functions.

What is enlightenment then? For *savikalpa* creatives, the discussion above has shown that the self-realisation experience requires a creative journey, but it is not the end of the road. You have to manifest the quantum self in your living; that journey is arduous. You have to literally *kill the me*, kill the ego-character even, more or less, as the traditions declare.

For the achiever of the *nirvikalpa samadhi* of the first kind, *turiya*, you would be co-presiding over the unconscious processing that includes the processing of supramental possibilities. This means that tuning yourself to the evolutionary movements of consciousness and acting from it appropriately would now be easy without effort. But there is still "somebody" who is walking his/her biddings in real time. A vestige of ego-identity remains.

Can there be a (unconscious) state of consciousness deeper than the unconscious processor of the quantum possibilities of the whole universe? What was before then? It was consciousness with no limitation imposed, not even the laws that govern the universe. There are no qualifications and there is nothing to process, a reason Buddhists call this state of consciousness the great Void and Hindus call it *nirguna*, attributeless.

So the situation is drastically different for a person unconsciously processing in the attributeless. There is no longer any "thing" to manifest, all desires (*vana* in Sanskrit) of manifestation is now burnt away. So, this is *Nirvana*, to use the language of Buddha, the state of no desire.

When *nirvikalpa Samadhi* of no attributes or qualifications is achieved, in a sense it is liberation, because since there is nothing more to be accomplished, there is no need to take rebirth. If liberation means liberation from birth-death-rebirth cycle, then liberation arrives with *Nirvana*. But if you have the exulted notion that liberation means total freedom, forget it. With embodiment, one cannot be totally free of ego conditioning; one cannot always be in arributeless nirvikalpa. Hence the wise koan: how does the Zen master go to the bathroom? A Zen master goes to the bathroom the same way as every adult, using ego conditioning. And whenever the ego modality is used, the ego identity has a chance to come back and play out, a crude reminder that you are not totally free yet.

So, in esoteric Hinduism there is the concept of liberation in the body—*jibanmukti*--that then is recognized to have some limitations. Only for liberation at death, there is total freedom called *bidehamukti*.

But then, *what is the use of such enlightenment?* Obviously, our great wisdom teachers, Jesus, Buddha, Anandamayi Ma, and the like did not go this route; they could not have completed "killing the ego;" that would have made teaching and lecturing impossible.

There is a wise guy in America sometimes seen in new age conferences about consciousness named Swami Beyondananda, a very funny guy. He makes fun of enlightenment by calling it the search for "beyond the beyond." But truly, this level beyond Turiya is beyond the beyond. Can you go there? Of course you can. But do you want to?

In truth, going through it all does serve a purpose. A very subtle one. Enlightenment of liberation—going the whole way—leaves these people no ego to serve the world, but they do serve. Their presence produces an effect called induction, locally and maybe even non-locally via healing intention. In the presence of a magnet, an iron nail becomes temporarily magnetized—induction. I have been in the presence of such people who can induce peace and have been temporarily blessed with peace; and they, in my reckoning, since they were teachers, did not even go all the way!

Why is a flower? It just is, and the world enjoys the fragrance.

The end of Enlightenment's journey is *Nirvana*
—Cessation of all desires.
When all your identity structures give way
To a profound fluidity,
Only then is there unending celebration.
Call it enlightenment if you like.
This bloom has no name, only fragrance.

Epilogue
The Quantum Worldview

I

A New Way to Look and Live: the Aspects of the Quantum Worldviw

Below I give a short review of all the important premises of the new worldview and let you be the judge if you want to try living them, emphasizing them, and finding out their usefulness for guiding individuals and societies.

The Quantum Worldview consists of the following 12 important aspects and applications; if you understand these, you will grasp the power of the quantum worldview, and even be able to use the power to avoid mistakes in living and be happy.

1. Nonlocality and Oneness

Quantum objects behave as both waves and particles. In the beginning, this seems paradoxical; indeed, for decades, quantum physicists used to call this wave particle duality a paradox: how can the same object be a wave that spreads out, be at more than one place at the same time, and also be a particle that is destined to be only at one place at a time?

But there is no paradox. Quantum objects are waves in a "domain of potentiality" outside of space and time and when measured, they are revealed as particles inside of the domain of space and time or domain of actuality or manifestation. In other words, the quantum waves are waves of possibility; their wave nature is revealed by experiments only after a little analysis.

How do you discern between the two domains? In the domain of actuality, space and time, objects communicate with signals. Signals can move only at a finite speed. In other words, there is a speed limit, the speed of light, 300, 000 km/sec. In this way, in space and time, communication is local, going through space taking time.

In the domain of potentiality, objects can communicate without signals, taking no time at all. What does that mean? Think about it. If things are instantly interconnected, isn't that what we call oneness.

So, there is potential oneness beyond our separateness that we experience. Does that knowledge empower you? It should. Spiritual traditions, especially Vedanta, are telling you about oneness for millennia except that some traditions make it a question of faith. But not Vedanta. Yoga is the epistemological extension of Vedanta with qualification (or *Samkhya*), the metaphysical basis of the quantum worldview. And now that oneness is scientific fact: both theory and experimental data back the idea. Scientific faith! Integration of science and spirituality! Isn't that empowering?

2. Consciousness is the ground of all being

The potential Oneness of the domain of potentiality in quantum physics is consciousness. Consciousness is the ground of all being and all our experiences in the domain of actuality or manifestation originate from this ground. How does this follow? You notice that whenever there is a manifest object in your experience, there is also a co-arising subject, you, looking at the object. So, the domain of potentiality must also have the potentiality of being that we call subject. A being that manifests as both subject and object is what we call consciousness.

Material possibilities are of two types. Most of them are reductive; they can be reduced to their base level, the elementary particles. They give rise to the part of the world that we find non-living and insentient. But there are also material possibilities in consciousness—namely, the living cell and the brain--that contain irreducible circular wholes, called "tangled hierarchies" with which consciousness identifies as it changes possibility into actuality. In this way, the living cell and the brain make manifest representations of consciousness in space and time acquiring a self. Consciousness identifies with these systems while changing their possibility into actuality. As a result, these systems have the self-experience of "life" separate from environment and "subject" separate from objects respectively.

In this way, this aspect of the quantum worldview gives a basis for understanding biology—the science of life as different from nonlife, and psychology—the science of the self and its experiences as different from robots and computers.

I hope you see the empowering thought here. You are not a robot; you cannot be reduced to your parts and constructed in the lab from non-programmed molecules or controlled in any other way. In psychological terms, the unmanifest ground is your unconscious, but don't be confused. The quantum unconscious is much broader in scope than what Freud or even Jung envisioned for our unconscious. Also, the causal power of the unconscious is no longer paradoxical as it was in Fred Alan Wolf's thinking: we create our own reality. This causal power of choice we call downward causation.

Do you see the potential power this knowledge gives you? Your subjective free will is not the ornamental epiphenomenon of the brain that materialists tell you; it has freedom to say "no" to your conditioning that makes you mechanical and determined. This is how you open up to the real freedom of choice that lies in your unconscious ground of being.

4. Multiplicity of Human Experiences: The Quantum Psychophysical Parallelism

The quantum worldview opens the door to a science of all our experiences. An experience has two poles: the experiencer (subject) and the experienced (object). Each of our experiencing (sensing, thinking, feeling, and intuiting) of objects begins as quantum possibility of consciousness to choose from; choice actualizes the multifaceted possibility into a unique actuality. There is the experience of the subject also.

How does this knowledge empower you? Materialists see the human being as capable of processing sensory experiences and mental information, processing that even a robot can do given powerful enough computing capacity. Today's materialist culture emphasizes sensing and information-thinking, undervalues feeling ("emotions don't exist"), and ignores intuition. This is a straightjacket you wear when you succumb to this false news. But you know what? You have the key to free yourself: your feelings, your own new meanings, and your intuitions. Explore them; now that we have a theory for all of them the exploration is no longer shrouded with mystery, and be free.

5. We have not one but five bodies and this leads to a redefinition of Health and Education, even Economics:

Each of our experiences (the four mentioned above plus the experience of a self of oneness making a total of five) comes from a quantum world of potentiality. As we manifest experienceswith the help of our physical embodiment, we develop a "body" in each of the potential worlds. In this way, we have not one—the physical—body, but five bodies: physical, vital, mental, supramental/archetypal in the form of higher vital- higher mental (also called soul), and the self of oneness (also calledspirit).

With a science of experience in your vocabulary you can see how your concept of health must include all these bodies, not just the physical body. As you learn to conceptualize this way, your concept of health changes from "absence of illness" to "presence of wellness." This positive attitude is empowering, you will see as you explore more.

When you grasp the multiplicity of your experiences, you also begin to see that our educational system must emphasize all four different kinds of human experiences each with the idea of exploring the huge potentialities of transformation, intelligence, and happiness: Sensing (Physical Objects); Feeling (Vitality); Thinking (Meaning); Intuiting (purposive archetypal or spiritual values such as Truth, Love, Abundance, etc.). The happiness that comes with sensing is gross pleasure. The other experiences lead you to increasingly subtler and subtler forms of happiness. The exploration of the self too leads you to happiness; in fact, to the most joyful and satisfying kind of happiness.

Right now, your education is way unbalanced toward material sensing and mental thinking. To make the situation worse, mental thinking that should involve meaning is reduced to information processing making the happiness content worse. This emphasis on the gross has led to a neglect of your artistic and humanistic dimensions, the part of you that seeks feeling, meaning, and purpose. In this way, unbeknownst to you, you are being short-changed. Instead of joy and happiness, you are experiencing boredom which you try to avoid with trivial pursuit; instead of living enchanted, you are living in the dullsville of ignorance. The quantum worldview revives the arts and humanities in your educational system opening the door to your re-enchantment with the subtle wonders of the world.

6. The Two Faces of the Self

The core of our self-experience is the tangled hierarchical quantum self of co-arising of the subject-object polarity of the event of quantum collapse. However, the vehicles of self-making—the cell and the brain—make memory as experiences happen. This has the effect called conditioning—a tendency for the self of these vehicles to respond to a stimulus in the same way as in previous encounters with it. For us humans, the conditioned self is what we call our ego-character. However, our brain is constructed in such a way, that the memory can be reconstructed for a period; this phase is called short-term memory. This ability to reconstruct memory coupled with the ability to be "conscious of being conscious (of our past)" enables us to act with various personas—programs of personality--in various situations. In this way we develop a simple hierarchical ego-character-persona, the head honcho of our personality programs.

How does this knowledge empower you? You now can be aware how the personalities can be used in "inauthentic" ways by many people, even you. And then you can begin your journey to be as authentic as practicable. Authenticity helps your relationships to grow and your creative ability.

7. Purposive Evolution of Consciousness:

In the quantum worldview, evolution is evolution of consciousness in manifestation. Conscious evolution is purposive consisting of both homeostasis and discontinuous (quantum) leaps. In the past, evolution of how you engage your mind has given you the instinctual brain circuits of pleasure and pain and the collective unconscious (of Jungian vintage) that you share with all of humanity. But evolution does not stop there. As Sri Aurobindo has emphasized, evolution's objective right now is to transform our rational mind to produce greater and greater embodiment of archetypal (spiritual) values. Moreover, the embodiment of the archetypes also happens in the body organs of the navel and the heart chakra and involves noble feelings at these chakras. When these feelings are integrated and lived with the meanings we generate via the pursuit of the archetypes through our mind and brain, we develop what traditionally is called the soul. Some of us have been active in this way of "soul-making" for many incarnations already. For us, it is our special responsibility to align ourselves to the evolutionary movement of consciousness and contribute to more intelligence on the planet.

Currently the majority of us are stuck with the materialist concept of the material body as all that our embodiment entails, and intelligence as measured by our IQ. Quantum worldview, in addition to the structural physical body gives us the concepts of a functional vital body, a functional mental body, and a functional soul body. The idea of evolutionary transformation from the current stage of the rational mind to the intuitive mind whose primary purpose is soul-making introduces us at the personal level to the concepts of emotional and soul-level supramental intelligence. In essence, this leads to the spiritual concept of integrating the brain—the seat of the rational mind and the cortical self—with the heart—the seat of love and the body's self, except that the quantum worldview also gives us practical ways of achieving this integration. Arriving at soul level supramental intelligence brings us the highest satisfaction and sustenance.

Arriving at supramental intelligence is the goal of *quantum spirituality*. Quantum worldview recognizes only one other state of more wholeness than this, but that state of mystical enlightenment, Turiya, is not an achievement, it is the doorway to liberation from all achievements.

8. Individual Development: Reincarnation and the importance of character

Quantum physics indicates that the part of our ego that we call our character—the ability to learn specific tasks and especially learning to learn—consists of nonlocal memory and involves quantum leaps; itis stored outside space and time and can be inherited as part of a universal *law of karma* by subsequent "reincarnations" after we die. Through these various human incarnations ourcapacity to creatively explore feeling, meaning and purposeful archetypes increases manifold. When we realize and fully grasp this aspect of the quantum worldview, we recognize death for what it is: a way station for the purpose of renewal.

Note also that besides nature and nurture, there are propensities from past lives that you can manifest in this one. Through memory retrieval and past life regression techniques, you can also get a sense of the purpose of your lives that in India we call *dharma,* and live your life with the bliss of purposeful exploration. Having a purposive life in the form of following dharma, to quote the mythologist Joseph Campbell, is to "follow you bliss." You will see.

9. Creativity and Spirituality: The Creative Process—do-be-do-be-do, in essence—is the real secret of manifestation

Quantum Creativity consists of a "discontinuous" leap from the known arena of the ego to the unknown arena of new quantum possibilities of the unconscious that then manifestsin the primary experience of an unconditioned "quantum self" beyond ego as a creative insight about the question of exploration to which the ego gives form. The passionate creative exploration of new mental meanings and noble feelings, archetypal purpose, and spiritual oneness, is fundamental to being Human, it elevates human free will to say "no" to conditioning to real freedom of choice from new quantum potentiality. Empowering, yes, "but how do I do it, how do I explore creativity and arrive at the fulfilment of my human potential?" you say. Using the creative process, that's how.

The quantum worldview gives us a creative process that agrees with empirical data and provides a viable universally usable technique for both outer novel accomplishments and inner psychological and spiritual transformation. The essence of the creative process, do-be-do-be-do is this. "Do" means focused engaging with the object of your exploration. "Be" is relaxing, doing nothing, so the "divergent thinking" you generate in the "do" phase is processed in the unconscious. Alternative "do" and "be" results in convergent thought, aninsight. However, the insight comes as a discontinuity of thought, a quantum leap, which you follow through with manifestation of an outer product or an inner new you.

In this way, I hope you now see that your intuitions and following them up with quantum creativity is the real secret of manifestation, the seven I's: Inspiration, Intention, Intuition, Imagination, Incubation, Insight, and Implementation. Now you can really "create your own reality."

You can choose health instead of illness, you can choose happiness instead of suffering; you can choose wholeness instead of fragmentation in yourself.

10. Creativity of the Vital

In yoga psychology, our feelings of vital energy are said to be associated with seven chakras and organ functions at these chakras. Creativity and creative process applied to the vital arena "opens" these chakras meaning that the associated physical organs begin to function at a higher level. For example, when the heart opens, we not only can partake in romantic and maternal love but also in unconditional love. In other words, the immune system temporarily suspends its function of defensiveness and imposing expectations of something in return.

In yoga psychology, vital creativity is shrouded in mysterious metaphors of *kundalini* and *kundalini* rising. Knowing the theory behind the evocative language should empower you to explore and embody noble feelings that people hithertofore have only talked about.

11. The Quantum Vision of Society: Hierarchy of needs

Finally, the quantum worldview gives us the following visions of our future society.

Human enterprises must involve satisfying the needs of all human experiences, from the most basic survival needs to the pinnacle of the need for self-realisation—the awakening of the idea that the self does not exist apart from oneness. In this way the quantum worldview supports the psychologist Abraham Maslow's work in the 1960's. This hierarchy includes but transcends material sensing and artificial computer information-centred thinking.

Why is this important? Under the aegis of scientific materialism, our life today is mostly centred around the economy and the field that supposedly governs it—economics.In most of the world, the economic theory used is capitalism in which there are two wings—production and consumption. The basic assumption of capitalism is this: if both the producers and the consumers are guided by their "numero uno"—*homo economicus*—interest, then if the market is free from any other influence (such as government), the invisible hands of the free market will establish equilibrium between production and consumption, stabilize prices, and even allocate resources among the various sectors of the economy equitably.

The problem is this: our "numero uno" selfishness often collides with the interests of the whole society—*homo communus*. Total disaster can happen if the interests of *homo communus* are ignored for long; the current global climate change is an example of that.

Quantum science gives us a new paradigm of economics: extend Adam Smith's capitalism from the material domain to all other domains of human needs--the vital, the mental, the archetypal, and even oneness itself. Production and consumption of these subtle needs changes the economy from a transactional "zero sum" game, give and take economy to a transformational economy of infinite possibilities. What does that mean? We focus on the archetype of abundance instead of material wealth and that makes all the difference and includes *homo communus* in the economic equation.

12. Social Relationships and the Vision of a Transformed Quantum Society: Quantum Activism

In the past decades of scientific materialism, our individuality has gained prominence over our community consciousness to a pathological extent. According to the quantum worldview, the I/WE of relationships, the I/WE of quantum nonlocality and tangled hierarchy must supplement our simple hierarchical individuality I/ME. In economics, as discussed above this translates as the integration of *homo economicus* (the selfish human of Newtonian vintage) and *homo communus* (the nonlocal human of quantum vintage).

In politics, in representative democracy, the problem is of how our elected representatives use their power. Do they use power simply to serve their constituents who elected them (which of course keeps them perpetually in power) or use their power to empower everyone including the people who did not vote for them? If we are transactional, then we want quid pro quo, give and take. This is a sure-fire way to polarize the society as we now are seeing in America and elsewhere.

In transactional politics, minorities and the traditionally powerless suffer. This perpetuates racism, sexism, the perpetually poor, etc. In India, even the party of the "others"—the Congress party, because of the influence of scientific materialism, try to solve the problem of discrimination via political correctness. This is still transactional; instead, this party and BJP, true to the quantum worldview, must opt for transformational politics. In Brazil, the problem of corruption of elected government officials can only be solved via transformational education of the electorate and electing leaders of transformation to government offices.

Finally, I now can tell the vision of the quantum worldviewfor you and our society. As you practice quantum living and transform, the society around you transforms through your example and through protracted use of quantum activism. Asthe use of quantum nonlocality, discontinuity, and tangled hierarchy become commonplace in our living, the whole society changes to a participatory community of individuals,a sort of quantum community of individuals guided by theirinner quantum self. The government still has a function, butit is reduced to a minimum; in that way the polarization as we witness today, between the two parties of representative democracy will disappear.

I hope even from this brief summary you can see that the quantum worldview does give answers to perennial questions of meaning and purpose, of life, death, love, satisfaction, happiness, intelligence, and even of spiritual enlightenment.It gives us the tool—creativity—for achievement of all human potentiality. It revives the arts and the humanities, generalizes the concept of health to wellbeing in all the different compartments of our being, and gives us new approaches to social sciences like economics and politics. All this I have written about elsewhere in my books. This epilogue is only a glimpse.

Further Reading

Aurobindo, Sri. *The Synthesis of Yoga*

Aurobindo, Sri. *The Life Divine*

Briggs, J. *Fire in the Crucible*

Chopra, D. *Quantum Healing*

Christ, J. *The Gospel according to Thomas*

De Chardin, Teillard. *The Phenomenon of Man*

Goswami, A. *The Self-Aware Universe*

Goswami, A. The Visionary Window

Goswami, A. *Physics of the Soul*

Goswami, A. *The Quantum Doctor*

Goswami, A. *Creative Evolution*

Goswami, A. *Quantum Creativity*

Goswami, A. *Quantum Economics*

Goswami, A. *The Everything Answer Book*

Goswami, A. *Quantum Politics*

Goswami, A. and Onisor, R. V. *Quantum Spirituality*

Goswami, A., Onisor R V. The Quantum Brain

Goswami, A. and Pattani, S. *Quantum Psychology Quantum Science of Happiness*

Jung, C. J. *The Portable Jung*

Krishna, Sri. *The Bhagavad Gita*

Maslow, A. *The Further Reaches of Human Knowledge*

Merrell-Wolff, Franklin. *Philosophy of Consciousness without an Object*

Merrell-Wolff, Franklin. *Philosophy of Experience*

Nikhilananda, S. (Tr.), *The Upanishads*

Penrose, R. *The Emperor's New Mind*

Searle, J. *The Rediscovery of the Mind*

Sheldrake, R. *A New Science of Life*

Stapp, H. P. *Mind, Matter, and Quantum Mechanics*

Tagore, Rabindranath. *The Religion of Man*

Taimni, I. K. (Tr.), *Patanjali's Yoga Sutra*

Wilber, K. *Up from Eden*

Wolf, F, A. *Taking the Quantum Leap*

INDEX

A

abundance, 10, 149
acupuncture, 78, 79
Aha experience, 102
amygdala, 84, 177
ananda, 2, 6
anandamaya kosha, 2, 91
archetype, 63, 130
ashram, 39, 172
aura, 121
Aurobindo, 61, 127
Ayurveda, 77

B

bliss body, 129, 130
Bhagavad Gita, 216
Brahman, 8, 60
brain,
negative emotionalbrain circuits, 177
brow chakra, 83, 88
third eye, 177
Buddha, 152, 201

C

chakras, 58, 74
chi, 78, 79
Chi Gong, 75, 79
Chinese Medicine, 78, 79
collapse, 35, 49
creative process, 113, 115
creativity,
fundamental, 98, 131
inner, 98, 153
outer, 98, 162
situational, 98, 137
crown chakra, 83

D

dichotomies, 171, 173
deva, 137, 138
danava, 137, 138
discontinuity, 102, 128
dharma, 130, 131
do-be-do, 111, 112
dualism, 8, 9
downward causation, 23, 24

217

E

Einstein, Albert, 22, 70
emotional intelligence, 85, 177
enlightenment, 18, 40
entanglement, 71
evolution, 74, 77

F

Fight/flight, 154, 168
five bodies, 129, 206
fMRI, 143

G

Gandhi, 153, 161
genes, 75, 97
Good-evil dichotomy, 171
gunas, 77, 78

H

healing, quantum, 172, 216
Heaven, 11, 12
hierarchy, simple, 20, 21
tangled, 46, 47

holism, 13
homeostasis, 208
hyperactivity, 137, 142

I

imbalance, 119, 125
immanent, 23, 32
immune system, 82, 83
incubation, 211
inner-outer dichotomy, 171
insight, 8, 42 *intelligence*,
emotional, 85, 177
mental, 139
supramental, 177, 209
intuition, 1, 2

J

Jung Carl, 17, 52

K

Kali, 144
karma, 12, 209
Krishna, 167, 216
Krishnamurti, 40,
Krishnamrthy, Jiddu, 40,

M

Maharshi Ramana, 86, 198
manava, 137, 138
Mandela Nelson, 161
mantra, 100
material body, 10, 60
materialism scientific, 4, 9
mental body, 99, 129
mental intelligence, 139
metaphysics, 42
mind-brain, 94
mindfulness, 189
miracle, 123
movement of consciousness, 148, 155
Moss Richard, 58, 74
mystic, 39, 40

N

nadis, 78
navel chakra, 81, 88 negative emotional braincircuit, 177
neuroscience, 3, 183
Nirvikalpa samadhi, 193, 194
nonlocality, 28, 35

P

Patanjali, 45, 194
Pattani Sunita, 140
persona, 180, 185
polarity, 180, 207
political, 161, 162
Precision Nirvana, 45
preconscious, 136
present centeredness, 40
processing, unconscious, 104, 107
program, 59
psychology transpersonal, 14, 15
yoga, 60, 82

Q

Quantum activism, 148, 214
healing, 112, 172
leap, 18, 102
self, 6, 49
thinking, 94, 110
spirituality, 173, 179
worldview, 24, 132

R

Radha, 167
rajas, 137, 160
reincarnation, 12, 64
root chakra, 82, 88

S

Samadhi, 182, 193
Nirvikalpa, 193, 197
Savikalpa, 193, 200
Samkhya, 60, 204
sattva, 160, 161
Searle, John, 56, 96
secret, the, 43
archetype, 63, 130
sex chakra, 88, 176
Shakti, 18
Shiva, 34
Sheldrake, Rupert, 58, 74
simple hierarchy, 20, 21
Sivananda, Swami, 197, 198
soul making, 158, 176
stomach, 81
subject-object split, 49, 50 supramental intelligence, 177, 209
synchronicity, 69, 129

T

Tagore, Rabindranath, 167, 179
tamas, 137, 160
tangled hierarchy, 46, 47 The quantum
science of happiness, 216
throat chakra, 83
transcendent, 23, 32
transpersonal, 14, 15
turiya, 197, 200

U

Upanishads, 1, 3

V

V-organ, 59, 75
Vedanta, 56, 60
Vital body, 6, 64
Von Neumann, John, 17, 37

W

Wolf, Fred Alan, 17, 37

Y

Yoga sutra, 217

Z

Zen koan, master, 18

AMIT GOSWAMI, PHD is a retired professor of physics from the University of Oregon where he served from 1968-1997. In 1985, he discovered the solution to the quantum measurement problem and developed a science of experience explicating how consciousness splits into subject and object. Subsequently, he developed a theory of reincarnation and integrated conventional and alternative medicine within the new quantum science of health. Among his discoveries are the quantum theory of the creative process, the theory of quantum evolution, the science of love and happiness, the theory of quantum economics that extends Adam's Smith's capitalism into a workable paradigm for the 21st century, and the theory of quantum spirituality based on the exploration of wholeness.

In 1999, Amit started a movement called quantum activism, now gaining ground in North and South America, Europe, and India. In 2018, he and his collaborators established Quantum Activism Vishwalayam, an institution of transformative education in India, based on quantum science and the primacy of consciousness.

Amit is the author of numerous books, most notably: The Self- Aware Universe, Physics of the Soul, The Quantum Brain (with Valentina Onisor), The Quantum Doctor, God is Not Dead, Quantum Creativity, The Everything Answer Book, Quantum Spirituality (with Valentina Onisor), Quantum Activation (with Carl Blake and Gary Stuart), and Quantum Psychology and Science of Happiness (with Sunita Pattani). He was featured in the movie What the Bleep Do We Know!? and the documentaries Dalai Lama Renaissance and The Quantum Activist.

Amit is a spiritual practitioner and calls himself a quantum activist in search of Wholeness.

Printed in Great Britain
by Amazon